the wise WOMAN within

JILL TRESEDER

*Gail
with best wishes
Jill Treseder*

StarDrum Books

First published in 2004 through StarDrum Books
by arrangement with the author
ISBN 0-9544956-4-0

All rights reserved
Copyright © 2004 Jill Treseder

The right of Jill Treseder to be identified as the author of this work has been asserted by her in accordance with the Copyright, Designs and Patents Act 1988.

Illustrations by Pauline Ellison

No part of this book may be reproduced or utilised in any form or by any means, electronic or mechanical, without prior permission in writing from the publisher/author.

A catalogue record for this book is available from the British Library.

Printed in England by J R Digital Print Services

StarDrum Books
PO Box 32 Lechlade GL7 3ZR England
books@stardrum.com
www.stardrum.com

"Our deepest fear is not that we are inadequate,
our deepest fear is that we are powerful beyond measure.
It is our light not our darkness that most frightens us."
Marianne Williamson[1]

DEDICATION

This book is dedicated to my husband, Hugh –
supporter, critic, proof-reader and cook extraordinaire –
who has encouraged me every step of the way,
kept my sense of humour alive and without whom
I would never have finished.

ACKNOWLEDGEMENTS

I want to thank the following people for the insights, support, contributions or guidance they have given me.

My family: my parents from whom I have learnt so much, Hugh for putting up with it all for so long, Robert and Tamara, Andrew and Alison, Jessica and Tim for their interest and enthusiasm, Oliver and Emily for arriving in the world, and a special thank you to Jessica for pulling me round corners I wouldn't otherwise have turned.

My friend Sara for her constant support and clarity about 'sodding bitty bits' over so many years.

All those friends and group participants whose stories have contributed so much, as well as the Bath 'Old PG' group, the Blue Moon women's group and the belly dancing group.

Vicki Noble and Katheryn Trenshaw for opening doors to the mysteries of earth and body knowing and of women sharing ritual.

Scilla Elworthy, John Baldock and Christian Chemin for their networking, and John for his advice, all of which moved me along the path to publication.

The team at StarDrum Books who have been a delight to work with: Sarah for proof-reading (so I thought I could punctuate!) and for her valuable comments on content. Pauline Ellison for capturing the spirit of the book in her superb illustrations. Pauline and Kookie for the cover design and Kookie for typesetting

and

Annie Tatham Mannall of Stardrum for being such an inspiring, positive and practical publication guide.

CONFIDENTIALITY

I am deeply indebted to all the individual contributors whose stories and experiences are included in this book and whose privacy is protected by pseudonyms.

CONTENTS

Introduction		1
Chapter 1	Building Bridges Between Worlds	13
Chapter 2	Through the Eyes of a Child	23
Chapter 3	Emotional Housekeeping	39
Chapter 4	Developing Personal Power	59
Chapter 5	Our Parents Ourselves	73
Chapter 6	Breaking the Mould	89
Chapter 7	Body Knowing	107
Chapter 8	The Magic of Menstruation	127
Chapter 9	Wisdom, Spirituality and Menopause	145
Chapter 10	Our Place in the Natural World	161
Chapter 11	The Silence of Women	191
Chapter 12	Making a Song and Dance	215

INTRODUCTION

Too often women allow themselves to be defined by others: parents, partners, children, managers and the media. We lose the habit of looking within to know who we are, and learn to present the pleasing or appropriate persona at the expense of our integrity. The result is a life of compartments, inner conflict and suppression of inner knowing. This fundamental splitting is the consequence of social attitudes to women over the centuries. How for instance can a woman feel that she can be a good mother and a sexy lover when these two are stereotyped as mutually exclusive? How can she command respect as an effective manager if she admits to making decisions based on intuition?

Being faced with dilemmas of this kind drains energy and confidence and can even threaten sanity. It is one thing for a woman to feel confident either by herself or among other like-minded and supportive women. It is quite another for her to keep hold of that confidence and act upon it in the mainstream world of family, friends and work. But the world needs feminine wisdom! This book provides both the inspiration and practical exercises for women to get to know their natural intuitive wisdom and use it effectively at a personal level and in the world of work. Personal and professional illustrations and case studies focus on the critical importance of women finding a voice in both these environments.

The Wise Woman Within reconnects us to traditional sources of feminine wisdom: past experience, body knowing and the natural world, while maintaining a firm footing in the multi-faceted world of work. Starting from the premise that we have lost our connection with the earth, with our bodies, and with the wisdom of the ancestors, it follows these three intertwining threads to explore how we can recover from this loss. It applies the learning that emerges to both personal and the organisational relationships.

I see the process of coming to write this book as a series of pebbles dropping into my pond and causing ripples. The first pebble was a question. At the time I was working as a management consultant in a corporate environment, as well as a number of other settings. The question was how to manage the emotional agenda in situations where there was a task to be completed, but when the emotions involved were getting in the way. Attending to the emotions might be inappropriate and was usually resisted. But if we ignored the emotions, they would sabotage the task because people were pre-occupied and their energy diverted.

What does such an 'emotional agenda' consist of? What was it that I was making space for, holding up and reflecting back to managers and workers in organisations? To couples stuck in relationships? To failing committees? To women building the confidence to return to work?

Let me give you some background to illustrate the dilemma in which I found myself.

TECHNOLOGY & EMOTIONS

Back in the 1980s I was surprised to find myself playing a part in developing an exciting new kind of computer programme called an 'expert' or 'knowledge-based system' that was sweeping the world of information technology at that time. Its purpose was to make the knowledge of experts more widely available. A simple example would be the sort of knowledge that sits on a CD in a car to help you navigate from one end of the country to the other or find a particular city street. Others had more sophisticated applications involving deeper, more complex knowledge.

The challenge was to interview experts, 'extract' their knowledge and encapsulate it in a piece of software. The role of interviewer turned out to be formidable. It involved mediating between many different ways of seeing the world in order to avoid misunderstandings and mistakes. This task fell to the computer programmers. These were highly intelligent people who knew all there was to know about the inside of a computer. But most of them were boffins – 'backroom boys', as well as some women, living in a world of machines. However, they freely admitted that if you showed them another human being and invited them to have a conversation, they would tend to run a mile.

This was where I came in, as developer and co-teacher of a course that combined technical and human skills. The first part of my job was to coach the would-be 'knowledge engineers' in fundamental social skills such as introducing themselves, establishing rapport and learning to listen. The second part addressed the emotional content of interviews, and turned out to be complex and uncomfortable, both for them and for me. The discomfort became the grit in the oyster that led to the writing of this book.

As you can imagine, some experts were jealous of their knowledge and wanted to hold on to the power it gave them. They didn't want the world to benefit and became defensive and secretive. Some were understandably suspicious of being exploited by technology they didn't understand, or of having their expertise misused. Others were so deeply immersed in their field that they expressed themselves in incomprehensible ways. Still others had so many years experience that their knowledge had become 'latent' and they neglected to explain the founding principles of their expertise. There were those who were too shy to begin to talk and those who were too passionate to stop. Some were rambling and some were lucid. Many believed that they 'knew nothing' and were still revealing new depths to their knowledge two days later.

All of these experts gave their interviewers, the knowledge engineers, two sorts of problem. First, they were forced to deal with emotions; secondly they were confronted with 'messy knowledge'.

On the one hand, the experts might be hostile, cynical, excited, anxious – and uncooperative if these states were not respected and managed. On the other hand, the knowledge engineers had to cope with their own emotions. Lack of confidence made them fearful and defensive and they didn't know how to vent their frustrations in the interviewing role. They were used to shouting at a machine or kicking its box when things went wrong, but they couldn't do that with a person.

To add insult to injury, if the knowledge engineers were successful, the volume of apparently shapeless knowledge they gathered would be overwhelming. It caused them to panic because it defied being tidied into the black and white, factual boxes they were used to.

It became clear that the knowledge engineers would have to step back from an exclusive focus on the task and learn some process skills. Without the underlying ability to manage their own and others' emotions, they would never be able to tackle the task of building the knowledge into a system. I therefore set out to teach them emotional competence (which is explained fully in a later chapter). The technicians generally were reluctant to admit the need to attend to the emotional agenda. A few exceptional people were interested and eager. Many were reluctant and some felt threatened and caste me as scapegoat for their own fears. They argued with the philosophy of the course, criticised the design of the exercises and were cynical about the emotional theory.

It was hard to maintain the courage of my convictions in the face of this opposition, especially in the early days. I was new to the world of technology, unfamiliar with the task-driven, male-dominated culture and inexperienced in the teaching or facilitating role. I needed to be strong in presenting the facts about the human side of the task, and do that robustly, lightly, and even humorously in order to create a safe space for learning. When my own insecurity caused me to falter, that secure space was threatened and it played into the hands of my critics, particularly as I was a woman. In the long term, the experience of 'graduate' knowledge engineers did much to persuade me that the effort was worthwhile. Many reported back that the methods and skills taught on the course were necessary and effective tools. Even some of the most recalcitrant students had the generosity to admit that their later success depended on taking those lessons on board.

In this and subsequent work in the corporate environment, I found myself holding the ground at the meeting point of a number of conflicting views of the world. My role became a bridge between the world of technology and the world of human interaction; between the world of logic and the world of emotion; between masculine and feminine ways of thinking and behaving. For several years I became preoccupied with "talking about the 'E' word (emotion) to men in dark suits", which was my shorthand for the clash of values involved. I became so absorbed in that world that I even identified with some male managers who were finding the culture stressful and acquired the nickname 'champion of the men'. Meanwhile I struggled to cope with my own emotions and survive as a woman in the face of these tensions.

A "FEMININE" WAY OF BEING

All of this taught me that, in many organisational contexts, it was considered indecent to refer to emotions. I would feel as if I had sat inelegantly and shown my knickers. But addressing that first set of ripples in the pond also taught me that we cannot leave our feelings at home or ignore them for long. The basic emotions of fear, anger and grief are a powerful force. They are a major part of conflict, resistance to change and breakdown of communication. They are also a major part of success. Our creative energy is tied up in this emotional agenda. So it is crucial to face the 'E' word and learn to manage its agenda constructively.

But that was not all. The second ripple of growing awareness revealed that the phrase 'emotional agenda' was a shorthand and catch-all for a whole way of looking at the world that captains of industry prefer to ignore. Such cultures view emotions with suspicion. They also discourage taking time to be reflective; respect for intuition; leading from behind through facilitative listening and encouragement; attaching importance to the process of *how* tasks are achieved; using humour and playful tools that encourage imagination and creativity; and respecting the body – not only for its wisdom, but also for its need for rest, refreshment and recuperation.

A third ripple brought the recognition that all these habits of behaviour tend to be seen as traditionally feminine. We do of course see these qualities in many men, and the 'wise woman within' is frequently to be found within a man. But they are not valued in hard-nosed or macho cultures where men who operate in this way tend to be sidelined.

Inevitably this book is written from a woman's perspective. This is partly because I am a woman. It is also because I am exploring these 'feminine' ways of being in the world. Are these ways of knowing natural to women? How much have we forgotten? How can we reconnect more strongly with them and own them? How can we maintain that connection in environments that are hostile to thinking and acting in these ways? These questions are not just for women. They have relevance to anyone who struggles in environments dominated by patriarchal ways, whether they are women or men. I hope that men engage with them too, so that women and men can explore them together in a spirit of inclusion and open communication.

Recently, recognition has been growing that a 'feminine' management style is more effective in the current climate of fast-moving change.[1] Managers are exhorted to get in touch with their feminine side as research shows that "people with soft skills make stronger leaders".[2] Management consultants like myself have been promoting this approach for years and its power is now beginning to show in the bottom line of companies that have adopted it. But although many companies are developing more dynamic and participative cultures, they still harbour pockets of resistance and there are still plenty of companies, and indeed families, who prefer a more hierarchical regime. But even in those cultures, a hunger for change is to be found not far below the surface.

It soon became apparent – and here the ripples started to make waves – that there was another more difficult word beyond the 'E' word. This was the 'S' word. To say I found myself holding a spiritual agenda may give a misleading impression, but no other word is adequate. This spiritual agenda has nothing to do with religion but relates to people's need to have a purpose in their work that goes beyond self-interest and the bottom line, a need to put some meaning into their activity and to bring another dimension to their lives and relationships. The words 'spirit' or 'soul' can have many meanings. More than a decade ago Anita Roddick of the Body Shop spoke in an interview of asking her staff what would *"make their spirit sing"*. Suzanne Penn[3] of Roffey Park School of Management describes it as being about *"a sense of belonging and individual motivation"*. Alan Briskin[4], who runs a masterclass called *"Bringing your soul to work"*, refers to being *"fully human"*, engaging with *"the contradictions and turbulence of life"* and being *"open to the possibilities of a higher self"*.

Awareness of these issues is growing. The world is waking up to the fact that it needs the qualities and skills that women have to offer, *"that the collaborative, egalitarian spirit so often shared by women should be more carefully nurtured in the work lives of all men and women"*.[5] Increasingly business journalism reports on the need for values and qualities in management that have traditionally been associated with women's style. Mediation services are coming to the fore in business, political, neighbourhood and family relationships. Organisations are expected to be ethical as well as profitable and there is a growing recognition that spiritual values have a place in the working environment.

RECONNECTING WITH THE FEMININE

I spent many years learning to survive in resistant organisations. It took a woman's workshop with Vicki Noble [6] among the sacred sites of Cornwall to shift my attention to what it meant to *thrive* as a woman. The contrast was enormous. In work I was immersed in an artificially lit, carpeted environment populated mostly by men whose chief priority was commercial success in a competitive economy. The culture was formal and restrained. Suddenly I was transported to live at close quarters with a large group of women of all ages and backgrounds. Here the prime focus was our physical, emotional and spiritual well-being. We sat on the floor by a log fire and talked, laughed and sang to a guitar. We studied astrology and worked with the Motherpeace tarot.[7] We walked out in the sun, wind and rain and tramped through gorse and mud to sacred sites where we took part in rituals. We engaged in a ceremony of drumming and chanting for healing and learnt what 'raising the energy' really means. One of the songs talked of passing through the 'crack between the worlds', and certainly we achieved that.

My whole focus shifted to give attention to an inner life. Connections were made between the earth, spirituality and being a woman that had lain dormant since I was a child. I began to feel whole, and it felt like coming home. For years I had shut the door on a spiritual life because I equated it with 'religion', which I had experienced as exclusive and deadening. I always came away from church services feeling angry and upset. It was only years later when I read Merlin Stone's *'When God was a Woman'*[8] that it occurred to me that this might be at least partly because that form of religion was exclusive of women. Now my challenge was to admit the 'S' word into my life and resume a long-abandoned spiritual journey. Writing this book has become part of that journey, just as reading it may become part of yours.

THE JOURNEY

The journey is one of coming to know who we really are. It weaves in and out of personal and public life, reflecting the way that we take our private selves with us into the working context, and that we cannot do otherwise. It seeks to demonstrate the link between the inner personal world and the outer world of action, to examine the importance of childhood experience to adult life, and the relevance of ancient wisdom to present-day problems. Through all these links we come to know that mind and body are one.

This journey is not the kind that proceeds in a straight line from A to B. It is a cyclical process that may seem erratic at times, the pattern and purpose only becoming clear when we look back. It is as varied as the course of a river on its way from its source to the sea. In the beginning it bubbles up from underground and seeps almost unrecognised through marshy grass until it becomes a small but noticeable stream spurting erratically downhill. It changes direction, is easily diverted by small obstacles, then gathers momentum and finds its own course. In the early stages it plunges suddenly into dark caves, through woods, down hillsides. Even when the terrain levels out, the landscape is still varied and each change of country and weather is part of the life of the river. When it reaches the sea there is turbulence before it flows into the integrating whole of the ocean.

It is an important part of our process to go with the flow of this river, learning to notice the state of the water and to accept the landscapes as facets of ourselves that need exploring. Let me explain what I mean by 'going with the flow'. This is not a question of drifting passively on the current, being tossed by every eddy or being washed up or drowned. It is a matter of careful attention to the nature of the flow, both in surrounding forces and within our own systems of ebbing and flowing energy. It is an attempt to achieve some resonance and synchronicity between those two inner and outer flows, a harmony that converts energy into synergy rather than draining it through repeated collisions and mismatches. This activity requires cultivating active attention, constant alertness and a sense of timing. When excellently done it looks effortless, as if the actor does nothing: like the surfer who takes off to ride the wave at the optimum moment; or the sailor who makes a fast passage by sailing *with* carefully studied tides and prevailing winds; or the expert group facilitator who appears to the unaware observer to be drifting passively. Passivity has no place in any of these activities.

The kind of knowing that we will gather on this journey consists of intuitively developed threads that we can weave together into a pattern. The threads, although different in colour and texture, blend together. They will be drawn from the experience of childhood, our relationships with parents and how these impact on our adult life (Chapters 2 and 5). Chapters 3 and 4 prepare the ground for Chapter 5 by mapping the emotional territory and showing how to manage emotions in theory and practice, with reference to personal and working relationships. Chapter 6 explores some common behaviour patterns and how to develop personal power. Next we engage with body and 'intuitive' knowing (Chapter 7), and in Chapters 8 and 9 attend to the experience of menstruation and menopause, potentially uncomfortable subjects because they are rarely discussed. My aim here is not to shock, but to uncover the meaning and power of this physical part of women's lives and to change its 'unmentionable' label. In Chapter 10 we take a breath of fresh air and explore our links to the natural world. Chapter 11 examines the different ways in which women are both silent and choose to be silent. It emphasises the importance of cultivating creative silence to make space for reflection. The last chapter focuses on giving expression to the wholeness of the self we have come to know, celebrating it with song and dance and planning to apply that understanding in our lives.

An inspirational dream makes a fitting end to this introduction.

In this dream I am walking in a bright green, sloping meadow. Halfway down I hear an amazing sound coming from the hillside— the most *indescribably* sweet music. The sound is coming from a spring rising from the ground. At the bottom, the meadow is so marshy that it is almost a river, with the grass long and bent over, and the singing water oozing up and running over the top of the flattened grass stalks with little bubbles.

All the water flows into a sunken tank with creatures inside it and on the edge. It takes a long time to figure out the distinction between them. Inside the pool there are beautiful grey fish like huge salmon, all smooth and silvery, nosing up to the side in a great shoal. Outside is a mass of sleek, grey cats, almost otter-like. Some of them are peering over the pool-side and almost nuzzling the fish, but there's no question of catching them. They are not only co-existing, but almost metamorphosing into one another.

The dream filled me with joy and hope. It symbolised to me the possibility of a reconnection with nature as the source of our being. I saw the spring of singing water as that sacred source flowing into the manufactured container of our lives with transformative effect. Creatures that had formerly been in conflict were able to live in harmony and understand one another, exchanging roles freely.

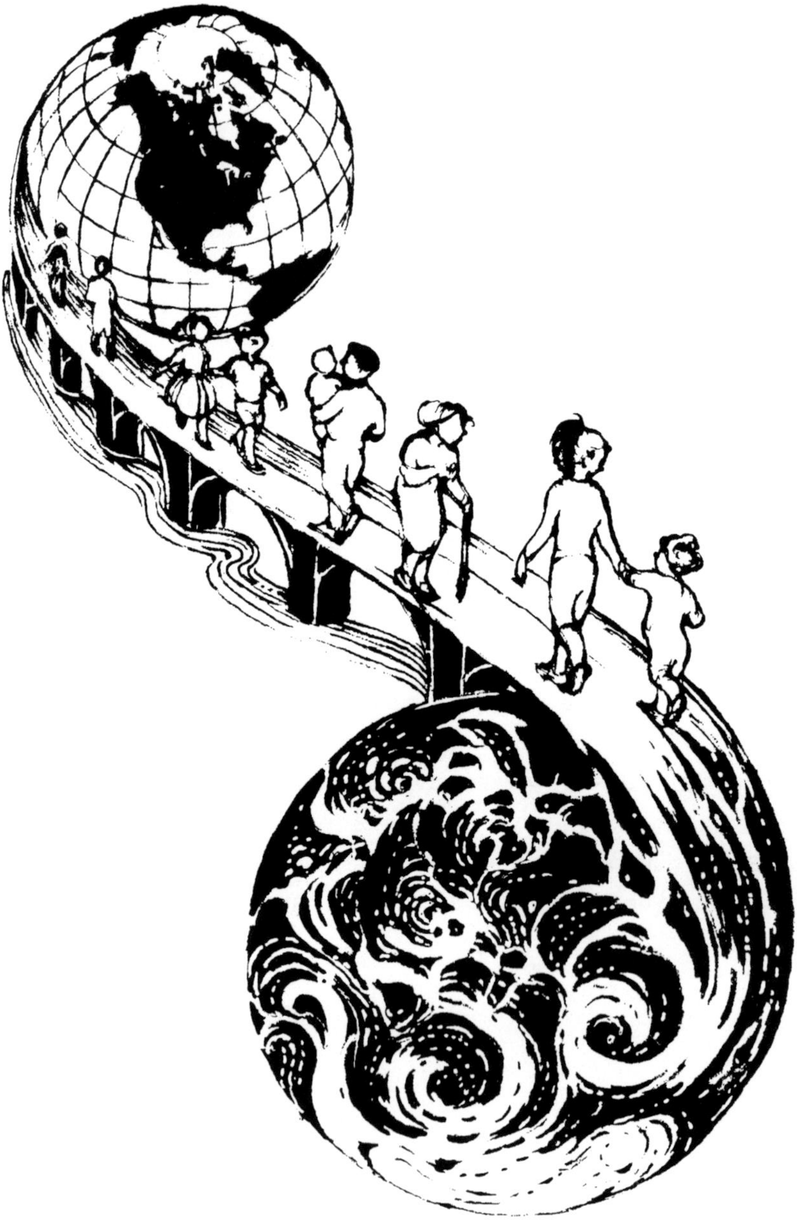

– CHAPTER 1 –

BUILDING BRIDGES BETWEEN WORLDS

"In the beginning, people prayed to the Creatress of Life, the Mistress of Heaven. At the very dawn of religion, God was a woman. Do you remember?"
Merlin Stone[1]

The policeman escorted me home and banged on the front door. It was 5:30 am and I was eleven years old. I had slipped out early that morning to see the sun rise over the sea from the beach near our house. The officer thought I had been there all night and clearly found my explanation as implausible as I found his suspicions. I was mystified and fearful at being walked back home by this inscrutable figure of authority. Next came deep embarrassment at the assault on the front door followed by shouts from the bedroom window. After all the commotion, my father's irritation melted into amusement and tea in the kitchen. By the time the police officer had gone back to his beat, my precious experience of the sunrise was on its way to a place in the family joke museum. Relief gave way to shame, and although I could neither understand nor admit it, I felt that something precious had been destroyed. And so I learnt, as many of us do, that secrecy and silence were the best way to protect such experiences.

That morning on the beach when the policeman came barging into my paradise, I left behind the age of innocence. It was a moment of truth, or rather of loss, of losing a direct connection to our natural spiritual source, a connection that is the key to our sense of wholeness: connection to natural elements and cycles; connection to the understanding held in our bodies; connection to the meaning of our past experience. It is the unifying pattern of all these threads that holds the secret of life. Maintaining a link to the child in us is vital, for children have not yet learnt the 'fact' of separation. They live in a connected world.

Of course years later, having been a mother and worked in the field of child protection, I am able to appreciate the policeman's concern. But I nevertheless grieve and rage that the need for such surveillance deprives children of their freedom as it did me. Whatever the policeman's and my parents' motives, the message I received was that my spiritual activity was not allowed, dangerous, an arrestable offence. That crucial, instinctive relationship with the spiritual source was broken. The encounter has echoes down the centuries from similar clashes between those who live in the world as a connected whole, and those who see a collection of parts that need managing and controlling.

A GOLDEN AGE

Imagine for a moment how that early morning experience might have been different. Imagine sitting by the water immersed in the swish and rattle of little waves on the pebbles and the intense colours of the sun creeping up over the sea.

Imagine that this is part of a normal waking ritual in a day that is regulated by sunrise and sunset, in a life that follows the seasons of the year. You know from the pattern of cloud in the sky and the colours of the sun what sort of weather to expect and therefore what the day will bring. If you are a mature woman you are also in tune with the phases of the moon that control your own cycle. You learn about herbs and healing and listen to your body to know what it needs. As a woman you are respected in the community for the sacred function of women in giving birth, for your deep connection to the earth, the tides and the moon. Women are at the centre of this community as priestesses, civic leaders and decision-makers. They are heads of household carrying the key responsibility of motherhood.

If you are a man you enjoy equal partnership with female friends and partners. You share the enjoyment of sports, dancing and religious rituals with women. You are neither dominant nor dominated, but live in harmony and collaboration with women.

This golden age is not a fairy tale. There is archaeological evidence that for thousands of years societies existed, in the Near and Middle East and Egypt for example, which revered women for their power to create life.[2] Names and inheritance passed through the mother, mutual respect existed between men and women, and worship was of the female goddess as the Great Earth Mother. The whole natural world was therefore held sacred and people lived according to the seasons, with respect for the elements and natural cycles. A close connection existed between the phases of women's life and the different manifestations of the goddess.

The goddess is a shape-shifter with three fundamental aspects of Maiden, Mother and Crone. Persephone, Demeter and Hecate are probably the most familiar examples of each of these aspects from the ancient world.

Today we recognise the Maiden in our inner Child, in spontaneous, emotional behaviour, imagination and playfulness, or rebellion. She is energetic, volatile, unreliable. She can be a delight and a pain, always unpredictable. Physically she is a virgin and she goes through a rite of passage when she first starts to menstruate.

The Mother is the mature phase of the goddess, nurturing and creative. Whether or not she is a physical mother, this woman is productive, achieving success in whatever field she chooses: from becoming managing director to bringing up children, producing works of art, fund-raising, cultivating a garden or caring for a dependent relative.

The Crone phase of the goddess corresponds to the time of the menopausal woman who keeps her blood inside to make wisdom. Traditionally, the Crone is no longer pre-occupied with success in the world and can turn her attention to spiritual matters. Crone probably derives from the carrion crow, sacred to the Death-goddess.[3] This links the Crone phase with old age, the waning moon and the decline and destruction that comes before rebirth and regeneration.

FROM CONNECTION TO FRAGMENTATION

Eventually however, warring tribes with very different values swept in from the plains of Northern Europe and destroyed the last of these civilisations in Crete.[2] Gradually a balanced culture whose values promoted peace, harmony, cultivation of the land, and creation of wealth and beauty disappeared. It gave way to societies where men held power, war was glorified, wealth was seized from others and women were seen as property.

This change was hugely significant. In the ancient tradition the earth and all of nature, the role of women, and the worship of the goddess were inextricably entwined. In the new order these were pulled apart. The earth was no longer revered, women and sexuality came to be considered unclean, and the sacred was represented by a fear-inspiring father god who was 'out there' rather than at the centre of life.

In the mythology of culture after culture we see the female goddess being conquered and replaced by a male god. The goddess religion became feared and went underground, although traces of it appear, sometimes in distorted forms, in the religions that took its place, such as Judaism, Christianity and Islam.

Take for instance the Genesis story of Adam and Eve in the Garden of Eden, a paradise that is reminiscent of the golden age. First the male god makes woman out of the man, reversing the long-established, familiar fact that man emerged from the body of woman. Then, appropriately, it is the serpent that gives Eve to eat of the tree of knowledge, the serpent being an ancient and sacred symbol of female regenerative energy. The punishment for the serpent is to be cursed and despised by the woman. The woman too is punished. She is estranged from the serpent, the source of her wisdom and power, and subjugated to the will of her husband. The earth itself is cursed and the couple banned from paradise.[4]

In Christianity women are presented with Mary who is recognisable as the Mother Goddess. But as Virgin and Mother, her contradictory attributes put her beyond the reach of all women. Women were once considered natural priestesses, and yet the ordination of women is still opposed in many churches across the world. When the old beliefs went underground many wise women passed on their knowledge of natural remedies and sacred rituals in secret. These herbalists, healers and midwives were considered to be witches, although their witchcraft consisted of using their knowledge of plants and their healing powers to effect cures. In the Middle Ages religious authorities were responsible for the burning of an estimated nine million women witches, the wise women of the time.

As Jean Shinoda Bolen says, *"somewhere in our souls"* we remember this time of persecution:

> *"This collective memory has an effect much as any personal repressed trauma does; it makes women anxious when we discover our own sacred experiences ... We need courage to bring forth what we know."* [5]

Where and how do we find this courage? Having seen what we have lost as women, spiritual beings and inhabitants of the earth, what are we to do about it? How can we aspire to live once again intuitively and in harmony with the natural world? How we can nurture our spirit and give sacred values a meaningful place in the midst of our busy-ness? How do we address these problems, not only in our personal lives but also in the context of the organisations in which we work?

We cannot turn back the clock. We cannot simply dismantle the complex society that we live in and return to nature. In any case it would be a mistake to assume that everything in the garden of the golden age was lovely. I am not suggesting that women are or were blameless, or that the fault lies entirely with men for the loss of harmony between humans and the natural world. Similarly, although there is much that needs to be remedied about the way we treat the earth, our civilisation is not all bad. Our tragedy is our loss of the natural wisdom that comes from understanding the cycles of life and death and that all things are interconnected. This includes a failure to link one phase of life with the next, one context with another, which means that we often lose or devalue the wisdom we have developed along the way.

The good news is that we do not have to make a choice one way or the other here. We do not have to choose modern science or natural wisdom. In fact if we are to re-establish a healthy balance, if we are to maintain or recover our wholeness as human beings, we have to choose both. Learning the skills of communicating across divides, living on the edge, and bridging the space between worlds that have differing values or views of reality is crucial to being effective in our complex society. It makes the difference between merely surviving and thriving in this world. But this is not easy. My experience of working as a consultant in organisations has shown me how supremely difficult it is for anyone to maintain their connection with the natural world and intuitive knowing in a technological environment. Furthermore, both female and male managers have problems accessing and valuing their natural wisdom when they are relentlessly interrupted by demands from the predominantly patriarchal world in which they work.

Take for example, the story of a Wall Street bank conducting research into the most effective methods of predicting market trends. A number of top financial analysts were interviewed and persuaded to reveal the systems they used. One of the most successful experts was inexplicably resistant. Eventually the problem was revealed. The expert was a woman, her method relied on intuition, and in spite of her well-established reputation, she believed she would lose all credibility if she admitted to this.

Think of times in your life when you experience conflict between your inner and outer worlds; when you choose not to voice your truth in order to avoid ridicule; when you are caught as 'piggy-in-the-middle' between people who cannot understand each others' point of view; or when you are in transition between two very different areas of your life.

Now try this exercise to explore what it feels like to be a bridge.

EXERCISE – BUILDING YOUR BRIDGE

Put some time aside – at least half an hour. Try to ensure that you will not be disturbed. Have a notebook and pens beside you.

Make yourself comfortable, either sitting or lying down and take some deep breaths. Check your body for signs of tension and relax muscles by clenching them tightly and then releasing them. Close your eyes.

Imagine a bridge. Take the first one that comes into your mind. You are that bridge.

Take some time to notice its qualities.

What is it made of? Is it old or new, high or low? What shape is it?

Is it wide or narrow? Weak or strong?

What is it bridging, why is it there? What or who travels across it?

Where is it located? What can you see around it?

What does it feel like to be this bridge?

Notice the sensations in your body and the emotions that come to you.

Now take leave of your bridge and open your eyes.

Make a drawing of the bridge or describe it in words, whichever you prefer. You may want to do both.

You can revisit this exercise at intervals, as I did, to see how your bridge changes over time. Once mine was tall and thin and wobbly, at another time it was almost hidden in dark shadow, and once there was no way to climb onto it. No bridge is right or wrong, it just is. Being able to see it may help you gain insight into what you might do to make the structure more effective and to give yourself support in whatever bridging activities are coming your way.

What would your Wise Woman do?

She would slow down and listen to the things not being said.

Then she would know what to do.

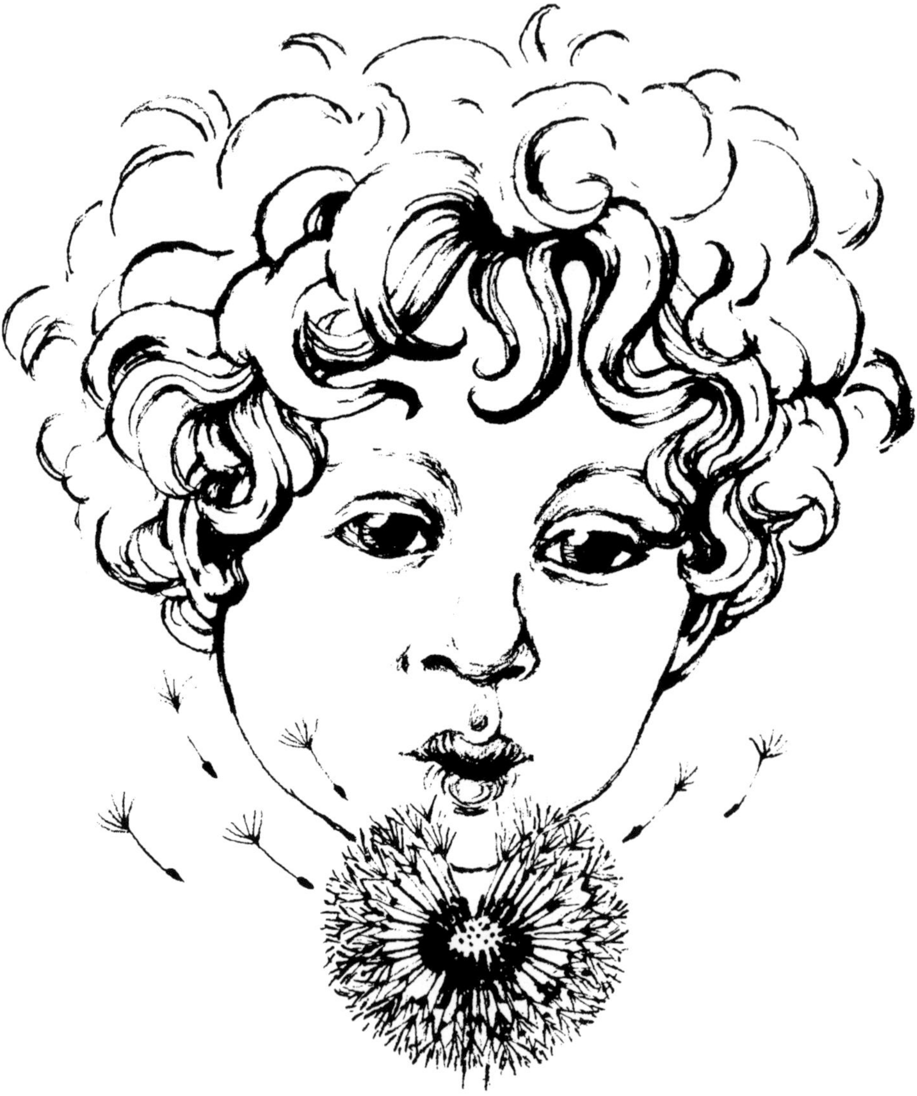

– CHAPTER 2 –

THROUGH THE EYES OF A CHILD

"Children do not give up their innate imagination, curiosity, dreaminess easily. You have to love them to get them to do that. Love is the path through to permissiveness to discipline: and through discipline, only too often, to betrayal of self."
R D Laing [1]

Sometimes as adults we find it hard to remember what it was like to see the world through the eyes of a child. Yet our spontaneous Child is still within us, a valuable source of playful energy, renewal and creativity. Through her we can make the vital links to the natural world, body knowing and the sacred. To achieve this we probably need to distinguish between the chronological child we once were, and the eternal Child we carry inside (referred to with a capital letter).

The Child represents the part of ourselves that is spontaneous and emotional. We have this part throughout our lives, but often neglect it in adulthood. The Child functions through physical sensations, emotions, imagination and intuition. She can be impulsive, rebellious and impatient, creative and irrational, naïve, dreamy and sensitive, funny and affectionate. The Child lives in the present, is unpredictable, and is uninhibited in expressing both negative and positive emotions. She relates directly to the natural world, representing the phase of the new crescent moon, a time of fresh beginnings, experiment and adventure.

She is also tuned in to the spiritual dimension. As young children we don't distinguish between 'reality', imagination and spirit. We readily see auras and communicate innocently with the spirit world because we have not yet been taught that this is difficult, or logically impossible, and are not yet distracted with adult preoccupations.

The energy and perspective of the Child in us is of key importance as we seek to achieve more wholeness and creativity in our lives. To recapture that perspective it may be helpful to recall places that were special to us as children, magical encounters, dreams or activities that held special significance.

EXERCISE – YOUR SPECIAL PLACE

Put some time aside – at least half an hour, preferably an hour. Try to ensure that you will not be disturbed. Have a notebook and pens beside you.

Make yourself comfortable, either sitting or lying down and take some deep breaths. Check your body for signs of tension and relax muscles by clenching them tightly and then releasing them.

Take yourself back to a special place that was your secret hideaway as a child. Remember what it was like to be in this place. What was it made of? What did it smell of? Were there other creatures or children with you there? When you stretch out your hands what do you feel?

If no secret place comes to mind then take yourself back to the house you first remember and imagine that you are in your favourite room or the room you used most. Use your senses as above to bring it to life.

Then come back to your body and draw it and write about your impressions.

THE OTHER WORLD

The Child is unequivocal about our need for a spiritual connection. Many people who set out to heal their inner Child experience a shift into another dimension, feel touched by a sense of universal love or tap into a different order of creative energy.

Neil was a student on placement in a high-tech company when he came on a three-day personal development course. He arrived in shorts, sunburnt from a weekend sailing and keen to participate in the programme. During an exercise, in which small groups of people were practising the skills of giving and receiving criticism and praise, he broke into deep sobbing. Commenting on the experience afterwards he wrote:

"I was feeling a huge, soft black and orange ball in my stomach. It seemed like an initiation ceremony onto the spiritual track of life which had been sliding away from me. The release gave me the sense of being Loved with a capital L and I am now able to recognise and accept myself in a new way."

I had an extraordinary reminder of the other world and the spiritual track. I was finding it difficult to admit that I needed a spiritual life. I had closed the door on religion years before, unable to accept the doctrines of the church which I found exclusive and punitive. I was in conflict. I felt an inner spiritual need, but was unable to say the 'S' word. It had too many off-putting associations. I had not reckoned with my Child.

My Child had the foresight at the age of thirteen to write a wise letter to my adult self, which she then hid in a writing case until it was the right time for me to find it again – thirty-five years later. It was a message from Child to adult, carefully dated almost as if it were a will. Very solemnly it aimed to guard against the possibility or probability that as an adult I would have forgotten the 'other world', and reminded me to stay true to it, come what may. I found the experience of reading this letter hard to describe. It was like looking in a mirror and seeing someone else, but someone who looked very familiar. Suddenly I came face to face with a 'more real' self.

The pages I found were headed *'Lovely feelings belonging to the other world'*, and evoked the 'other world' in sensual terms typical of the Child: *"the feeling of being thirsty and wanting a lost drink"*. It explained that the drink was lost *"because you are too old."* The letter referred to *"the feeling in your bottom tummy when you watch the sea very rough and grey"*, coining the phrase 'bottom tummy' that maybe you will find as useful as I have in locating your own inner knowing.

My Child also described *"the feeling of going back"* which she clearly thought would need some explanation to the adult world. This is a question of finding time alone, taking ourselves back as far as we can and allowing ourselves to open to the feelings that come.

The letter ended with an emphatic message to the adult me which is relevant to us all:

> *"This is all to remind you when you are grown up and getting staider. The 'other world' is an imagination dreamland. If you think hard you will get a feeling like familiar strange childhood, and think harder still and you may get a glimpse of it. Read these notes to remind you ... Don't get old. This was you writing this in Jan 1958. You are still yourself."*

The idea of 'going back' seems key to the question of why my Child wrote those two pages and to the purpose of this book. As children on the brink of the teenage years we can identify something infinitely precious at a time when it seems to be under threat. The threat is two-fold, coming partly from the adults in our life and their (adult) way of seeing the world, and partly from the natural process of growing up. For we stand on a threshold, not so much aware of a door opening ahead of us, but of the door of childhood closing irrevocably behind us. At this time we are still able occasionally, and with an effort of will and imagination, to hold that door open.

My response to reading these pages was one of respect and gratitude, a sense of being cared for by my young self and entrusted with her wisdom. She was truly a messenger *"from a world we once deeply knew, but we have long since forgotten"*.[2] The letter is a reminder that we all have an inner wisdom that we can tap into at any time. Even when we forget, we have another chance, and another. It is always there if we look inside.

Why do we forget important things like that other world? When I look through old journals I am surprised again and again to find accounts of seemingly unforgettable experiences and insights. How could I possibly have forgotten them? Maybe it is necessary that we forget, if we are already fully stretched in our lives or attached to living a quiet life. For the experience of the sacred is too momentous to remember and remain the same person. Another reason for forgetting may be that the reminder of wholeness and connection is too painful when we live with so much separation in our lives. Eventually enough messages accumulate that they cannot be ignored, or a particularly powerful, or critically timed message gets through in a way which permits no forgetting, is witnessed, shared, and becomes part of our acknowledged experience of the world. Doris Lessing subtly and powerfully conveys this kind of awakening in *Memoirs of a Survivor*. Her metaphor is a solid wall where the wallpaper pattern shows through the paint, which gradually dissolves in the sunlight, until her character is regularly passing through into the rooms beyond the wall. The character speaks of her mental process:

> *"... the consciousness of that other life, ... was a slow thing, coming precisely into the category of understanding we describe in the word realize, ... a gradual opening into comprehension. ... And of course one can 'know' something and not 'know' it. (One can also know something and then forget it!)"*[3]

YOU ARE STILL YOURSELF

The part of us that still inhabits the 'once upon a time' golden age of early childhood is sometimes called our 'Spontaneous Self'. Some of us find it hard to identify with that self for she may differ from the child we remember being.

Take the example of Anita, a woman in her fifties who was a member of a women's group. She recalled being a self-conscious, sulky child. So she was puzzled by photographs and family stories that portrayed her as happy, loving and playful. When invited to 'get in touch with her inner child' and be playful during group sessions, she would stand on the edge or hide under a table. It was the same with party games. Anita found it hard to let her hair down without the help of alcohol and would retreat to the kitchen. She couldn't find her Spontaneous Child.

Then quite unexpectedly, Anita encountered her during an exercise at a chanting workshop in a roomful of other people.

> *"We were told to close our eyes and chant our own name, over and over again, experimenting with all possible shapes and sounds of the syllables. The sound just took over after a bit. It became very urgent and painful. It was like a search or a quest. I was running after this little girl. She was very confident and carefree, a blonde-haired child. She ran along a ridge and stopped to play under a tree. I felt desperate. I called out to her, Ni-ni. That was the name I used to call myself as a small child. But 'Ni-ni' ignored this, she seemed to be in a world of her own. I was sobbing with a great longing, but when the child in my vision eventually turned round, she looked right through me as if I was invisible."*

This glimpse of an identity that was lost happened at the end of two intensive days of sound and vibration using hitherto unknown or unused channels. Anita came out of the exercise drenched in tears and sweat, feeling breathless and exhausted, and overwhelmed by a sense of loss and desertion. It caused her such intense pain that it even occurred to her to wonder whether she had had a twin sister whom no-one had told her about.

The power of Anita's experience convinces me that our history is indeed encoded in our bodies. The body holds the memory which may have been suppressed by the conscious mind following a traumatic event, illness or painful experience.

Nina's story reinforces this view. She found her Spontaneous Child through dance. Nina belonged to the same group as Anita, but reacted to play sessions in very different ways.

> "As a child I was a bossy little girl who always wanted to take charge. I knew the best gossip and I poked fun at other children who didn't do what I wanted. I get straight back to her, to that personality when I get into my Child."

It was as if this charismatic but rather spiky personality was picking away at the wounds that concealed the deep creativity of her true Spontaneous Child. She chose to dance as a ritual expression of herself in the final ceremony of the group. The beauty of Nina's soul dancing took everyone by surprise and touched the hearts of everyone present. As another group member recalled, *"she expressed happiness, anguish, pain, deep exhaustion, awakening, surprise, delight, ecstasy, power, strength, anger, grief, lyricism, wind, light, water, trees, stones, mystery, spirit and union. It was a dance of all our potential."*

However, we spend most of our time living in ways that shut out the Spontaneous Self. We busy ourselves with practicalities, function at a head level, and rarely choose to activate the physical channels that give access to re-membering that self. When we do, we attach little conscious weight to the results. This is even more resoundingly true in the business world. The idea of a healthy mind in a healthy body is ancient wisdom, but we either pay lip service to it or ignore it while indulging our addictions, whether they be to alcohol or work. At another extreme we concentrate on fitness, also to the point of addiction, which is not sane, healthy or even natural. Neither approach makes space for the deeper implications of health or wholeness. But however much we neglect, ignore or abuse our bodies and our feelings, we are inescapably physical beings. We become distanced from our bodies through a process of splitting.

THE IDENTITY GAP

The identity gap is one of the first major splits we experience and is well documented in child development literature. It involves losing the strong connection with the Spontaneous Self, described above, and gaining awareness of our Self as distinct from other people. This transition is part of growing up and becoming an individual. Before this we are a bundle of sensations. We have a view of the world that does not distinguish between the Self and our surroundings, and in particular our mother figure.

Tracking early memories confirms that self-recognition comes in dribs and drabs, becoming established by the age of four. Very early memories register in the body tissue and are only usually accessed in altered states of consciousness involving deep body work or hypnosis. At the next stage, we may be able to catch wisps of pre-verbal memory. These fragments have a dreamlike quality, dominated by sensory impressions of noise and shadow. The impact of sudden or intense sound, light or smell is probably what made them memorable.

As we grow older, the 'picture' becomes more focused and appears to cross some threshold. For instance, I can sometimes capture a blurry, mysterious impression of light and shade, shock and noise, which is associated with being in my pram in a thunderstorm. But a later memory is qualitatively different. It is a clear cut, colourful snapshot of finding toadstools with my mother when I was about two years old. This counts as an 'official' first memory because it sits firmly in the daylight dimension of everyday and is shared by my mother who is able to locate it in time and place.

A year or so later the split seems well established. I am rebelling against my mother's choice of dress and have an image of myself in the mirror wearing my 'fat dress', a hated flowery smock. This memory is different in an important respect. I am included in the memory picture, evidence that I knew then that I was separate. What is more I didn't like what I saw in the mirror and was in conflict with the most significant other person in my world. In giving in to my mother's choice of dress I am about to forfeit my Spontaneous Self, in return for mother's approval. This will establish a repeating pattern, common to many of us, which starts innocently enough but which has grave consequences in adult life.

Our potential for staying connected to our Spontaneous Self never goes away. When the pain of disconnection becomes too great, it breaks through our defences to remake the link. If this happens, the connection does not become whole and strong straight away. It builds, just as it broke, in fits and starts over time. We forget the connection, then re-member it, and grow it some more until it is strong enough to be a continuous thread in our lives. So Neil's spongy ball, my letter, Nina's dance and Anita's Ni-ni are only the first step of a journey of remembering. Although we may lose the connection many times and over long periods in our lives, we rarely lose the consciousness of that loss completely. Although we may not recognise why, part of us mourns the loss of the spontaneous self and the sense of being one with the natural world and we become restless and searching. Without it the part of us that we call a soul starves.

These examples illustrate the effectiveness of the splitting process. My letter that was 'lost' for thirty-five years is a remarkable example of this process of loss and rediscovery. My adult might have forgotten, yet, as a child of thirteen, she seemed aware of a further split about to take place, which would take my attention right away from such memories. The letter provides a vital link in the chain of re-membering.

> EXERCISE – YOUR EARLIEST MEMORY
>
> Put some time aside – at least half an hour, preferably an hour. Try to ensure that you will not be disturbed. Have a notebook and pens beside you.
>
> Make yourself comfortable, either sitting or lying down and take some deep breaths. Check your body for signs of tension and relax muscles by clenching them tightly and then releasing. Feel your weight on the floor, soften your eyes in their sockets and your tongue in your mouth and open your senses.
>
> You are going to connect with the earliest time you remember from your childhood. Memories become embellished by family anecdotes and by subsequent familiarity with their physical context. Screen these out by tuning in to body and sense awareness. Move your consciousness into your belly and notice what emerges.
>
> How old do you think you are? Where are you? Who is there with you? What are you doing? Choose a codename for this memory that will help you recall it – e.g. "fat dress", "toadstools".
>
> Now scan for another memory, earlier maybe, and do the same.
>
> Continue until no further memories come readily into consciousness.
>
> Then come back into present time and record everything you can recall. It is often best to start by drawing – either the scene or an impression of the emotions that you felt.

> Often memories will be about some kind of transitional time – the feelings involved make them more memorable. If this is true of any of yours, what was the nature of the transition?

PRETENDING – THE WORLD OF MAKE-BELIEVE AND FANTASY

Jan spoke to me when she was in her forties and at a turning point in her life. She had come to accept that, in spite of a happy childhood, there had been difficulties which she had a right to explore. Her story illustrates how easy it is for a child to lose a sense of identity and independence through the normal process of growing up, so that, even when there is no kind of trauma involved, there is still work to be done to recover wholeness.

"My childhood was happy and uneventful. I was an only child with a big garden to play in and parents who both loved me.

"My father worked abroad a lot when I was small. I remember one time he came home and I didn't recognise him. He was a bit of a distant figure but he used to read to me at bedtime and I loved that.

"The closeness was with my mother who coped with a lot of physical hard work in a big, cold house when we were on our own there. We had a lot of shared rituals for everything. She cooked and I helped, she made all my clothes, invented games. Quite claustrophobic really. We hardly ever saw anyone else. It was as if we pretended the world wasn't there. That must have been hard for my father to break into. But we needed him really. To bring the world in, to make it safe to go out.

"I was OK if I did what mother approved of. She was very controlling but subtle with it. It was a safe little cocoon with no conflicts – at least not on the surface. Years later she described me proudly as a child who never had a tantrum. It says it all really. It taught me not to think for myself. That was the condition for being loved and approved of I suppose."

This is a deal that so many of us make as children, and it costs us dear. It costs our independence, self-confidence and above all our very spontaneity.

Escaping into an imaginary world of pretending seems an understandable way of avoiding confrontations. It is also a way of maintaining healing contact with the Spontaneous Self who now seems to appear as a fantasy figure, separate from, but very real to the child. No wonder children are so reluctant to be drawn away from their make-believe games; no wonder Anita wept when she glimpsed her lost Ni-ni.

There are a number of different kinds of pretending. These can be illustrated by the series of invisible friends we invent as children. First there are the spontaneous products of our imagination, the shadow companions of the pre-school years. They go everywhere with us between the ages of about three and four and tend to be very vivid memories in that we can still 'see' now what they used to look like. These creatures must be important in charting our relationship with visibility, marking a transitional stage in the inner self becoming hidden. Next come companions more consciously invented to fill a gap, and make-believe games that deal with current experience like doctors and nurses. These activities give way to games that are almost role-plays with the function of practising for future occasions. I remember, for instance, playing 'Pauline and Ronald', a sophisticated form of Mothers and Fathers invented by my friend when she developed an interest in boys. Another friend worried her parents by insisting on playing with dolls when she was sixteen. For her it was preparation for life: she married straight out of school and had her first baby within the year.

This progression shows the shift that takes place as we get older – away from the magical and towards the practical. But if we were lucky as children, we will also have been initiated into the world of myth and fairy tale peopled by gods and goddesses, heroes, witches, trolls and animal helpers. This will have given us a grounding in magic and mystery that will stand us in good stead. We don't need to understand the symbolism of these stories for them to nurture the soul. Clarissa Pinkola Estés states, *"stories are medicine"* and *"soul vitamins"* and she tells us, *"we need only listen"*.[4] It is as if this listening that we do as children unconsciously gives us a template for deepening our understanding of our later life at a symbolic level.

How different from these personal fantasy worlds and powerful archetypes are the let's-pretend games and stories instituted by adults to calm and confine children. Tommy Worm who wears his vest in winter and the elves who always tidy away their toys may be useful allies for parents, but they do nothing to expand the creativity of children. They merely tie them to the mundane safety of mother's apron strings. Here are no rich metaphors or mysteries, no bad fairies or witches, nothing, in short, which might remotely risk giving a child a nightmare. These games can become almost a substitute for reality, denying the unfamiliar or the unpleasant. The effect of such a make-believe world can be to avoid the dark or frightening side of experience, which Jung called the *Shadow*, the world of deep feelings. Out of this may grow the habit of erecting a façade and of not allowing feelings to surface.

We need to stay tuned to our ability to believe in our inner world of imagination. Keeping that connection alive is vital. We owe this as much to our own inner Child as to the children growing up around us. Brian Patten's poem, *The Minister for Exams*,[5] speaks to both adults and children of the dangers of neglecting this dimension of our lives. He describes the ease with which a child can answer such 'simple' examination questions as *"describe the taste of the moon"* and *"what colour is love?"*.

*"I described the grief of Adam when he was expelled from Eden.
I wrote down the exact weight of an elephant's dream."*

He asks why, as an adult, this same child is sweeping streets and cleaning toilets. Why did he fail his exams? He answers with two further questions:

*"Q1. How large is a child's imagination?
"Q2. How shallow is the soul of the Minister for Exams?"*

EXERCISE – THANKING YOUR CHILD

Put some time aside – allow yourself at least one hour of uninterrupted time. Try to ensure that you will not be disturbed. Have a notebook and pens beside you.

Make yourself comfortable, either sitting or lying down and take some deep breaths. Check your body for signs of tension and relax muscles by clenching them tightly and then releasing. Breathe deeply to relax yourself and become present in your body. Close your eyes.

1. Choose a happy memory from your list of childhood memories recorded earlier – something that is both vivid and carries emotional significance of some kind. It may well be the first memory that came into your mind.

2. Allow yourself to sink into that memory and feel what it was like at that time. Notice your surroundings and the people present. What can you hear? Can you smell or taste anything? What is the texture and colour of the clothes you are wearing? Are you happy or sad, frightened or angry?

3. Open your eyes and start to write about the experience. Use the phrase "once upon a time" if it helps and write without reflecting or censoring. Just keep your pen moving without thinking too much about it. No-one is going to be marking out of ten. It is for your use only. Write for about 5 or 10 minutes. Then read what you have written out loud to yourself.

4. Take some more time to write your responses to the child you once were. You may prefer to do this on another day, giving yourself time to absorb the experience. Thank her for what she did for you at that time. Comfort her if she needs it. Think of ways in which you can protect your inner Child when she feels threatened by events. Write a list of these.

5. If writing is not something you enjoy, then find another way of expressing this memory. It is not supposed to be a chore. Try drawing or painting, or if you are more expressive with your body, choose some music that fits the memory and dance how you feel. Whatever you do, take some time to reflect on the activity afterwards and record your responses in stage 4 of the exercise.

What would your Wise Woman do?

She would slow down and ask the Child within her.

Then she would know what to do.

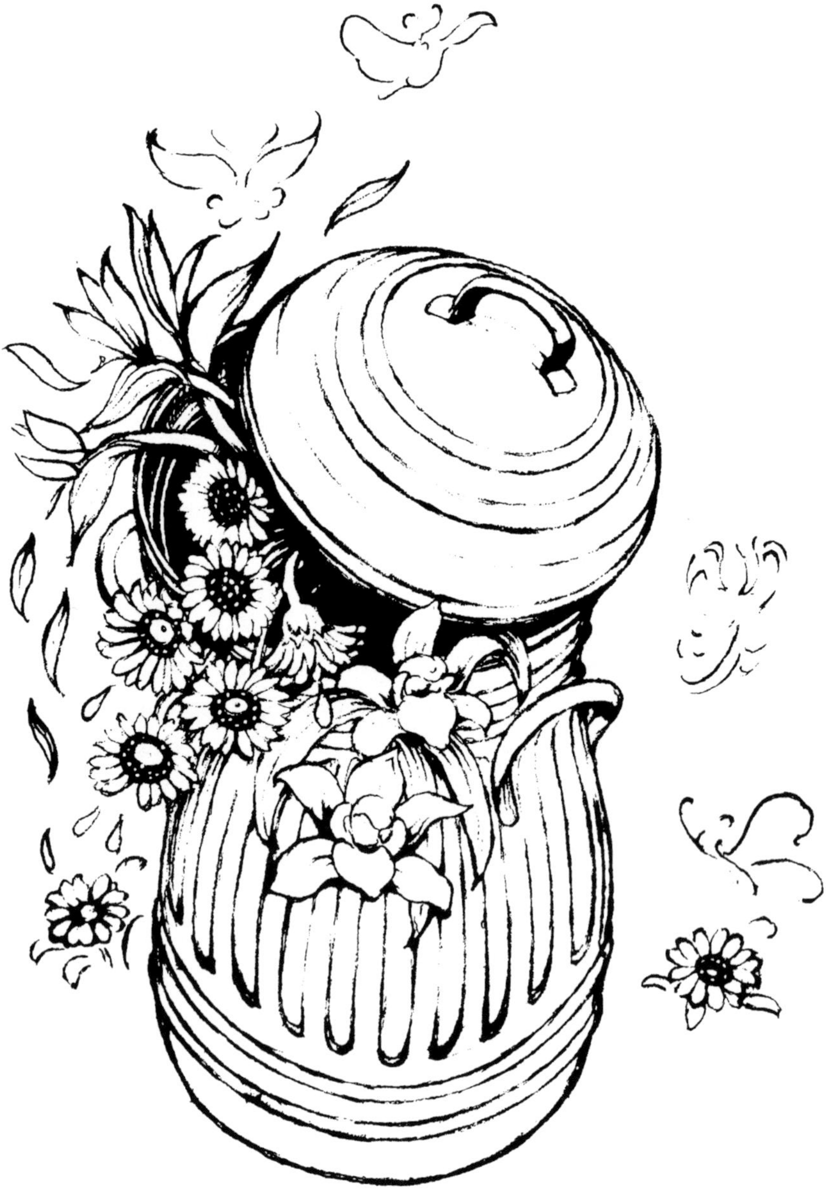

– CHAPTER 3 –

EMOTIONAL HOUSEKEEPNG

"Your joy is your sorrow unmasked …The deeper that sorrow carves into your being, the more joy you can contain."
Kahlil Gibran [1]

Little children are good at the spontaneous expression of emotion. They wail or rage, get it out of their system and are ready to move on. But adults in our society are not generally very good at managing emotions. Various myths abound concerning different nationalities. Italians are supposedly emotional and volatile. Californians are meant to be emotionally 'aware' and terribly intense because they are all in analysis. Whilst the English, especially men, and most especially those who went to public school, have a reputation for being so 'unemotional' that they wouldn't know an emotion if you dropped it on their toe. These myths are misleading not only because they encourage unhelpful stereotypes, but also because they confuse being unemotional with being emotionally controlled. There is a further confusion between controlling emotions and managing them. Control is only one skill amongst several that we need in order to manage emotions effectively. Control may be useful for short-term survival but *on its own* it is both psychologically and physically unhealthy in the long term.

So much that is precious is tied up in emotions, and yet we are afraid of them and lock them up in a kind of Pandora's box. If we cannot admit, understand and use our emotions, we will have difficulty achieving fulfilling relationships, being creative or even enjoying life to the full. On the one hand we shy away from so-called negative emotions like sadness and anger; on the other we are inhibited about expressing positive emotions like joy and excitement. Yet emotions give us the light and shade, heights and depths in our experience. They are evidence that we are alive, that we care and that we are both loveable and fallible. When we fear that showing our emotions may be risky, we need to remember that repressing them is not only unhealthy for us, but may also be hurtful and frustrating to others. If people close to you have tried shaking the feelings out of you, or have waved at you as if from a great distance, saying "is there anyone in there?" then you know what I mean.

HUMAN NEEDS

So what are the emotions we are talking about? We have six basic emotions: three positive, and three negative. Other emotions are compounds of these, just as colours are mixed from the three primary colours of blue, red and yellow.

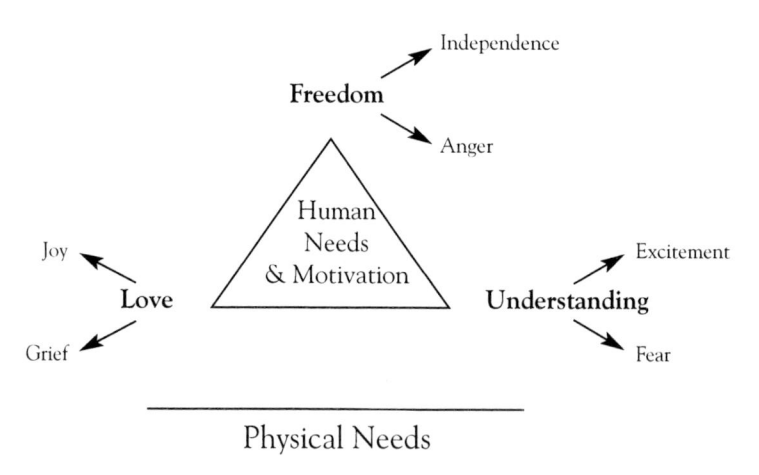

```
                          Independence
                        ↗
              Freedom
                        ↘
                          Anger
              /\
             /  \
            / Human \
    Joy ↖  / Needs   \  ↗ Excitement
          /& Motivation\
         /_____\
       Love            Understanding
    ↙                              ↘
  Grief                              Fear

            _____
                Physical Needs
```

The basic emotions spring from three fundamental needs or motivators – for Love, Freedom and Understanding (see the diagram above). These are psychological needs over and above the physical necessities of food, drink, sleep, shelter etc. When these needs are met we experience a positive emotional state and high energy. When these needs are not met we experience negative emotions that drain our energy *if they are not expressed*. Each of these needs involves giving and taking. That is to say, we need to be loved and to love; to understand and to be understood; to claim our own freedom and to accept that other people have freedom too.

Our need for love is basic to healthy self-esteem. Babies and small children who don't receive enough loving contact do not thrive as they should, even if they are physically nourished. Such children are likely to grow into vulnerable adults with low self-esteem. Healing these wounds is a process that may take years and depends upon learning self-love, which Gael Lindenfield describes as *"the essential food of the whole programme"* which *"must be administered immediately and abundantly in very practical and clearly demonstrable ways"*.[2] Gael is a psychotherapist who has developed a sensitive and systematic approach to emotional healing by coming to terms with her own difficulties. Even if we were loved as children, most of us still need to learn to love ourselves in order to cope with situations and relationships that undermine our self-esteem.

The need for understanding is about making sense of the world and developing a healthy curiosity. To do this we need information and knowledge, to be able to learn and to communicate with others. A child's understanding grows best if the world is presented gradually in digestible chunks, which are neither overwhelming nor over-protective, and which progressively develop confidence. As adults, we often find that the challenges that inspire most fear lead to the greatest rewards. Pushing through the fear is the secret, as explored in Susan Jeffers useful book, *'Feel the Fear and Do it Anyway'*.[3]

In a similar way children grow into their freedom needs. Too much is frightening, too little suffocating. A wise parent knows where to draw the boundaries and that boundaries are important. There is nothing more disconcerting than to kick hard against a wall and have it collapse. On the other hand, being imprisoned either destroys an independent spirit or causes it to flare into violence. By being granted appropriate freedom, a child learns to take responsibility, confidently claiming her rights at the same time as accepting the need to fulfil the corresponding obligations.

In the diagram below, the three fundamental needs have been expressed in ways that are more easily open to discussion in the work environment as well as in a personal context. Love has been replaced by Respect and Appreciation; Freedom by Choice; and Understanding by Communication and Clear Objectives.

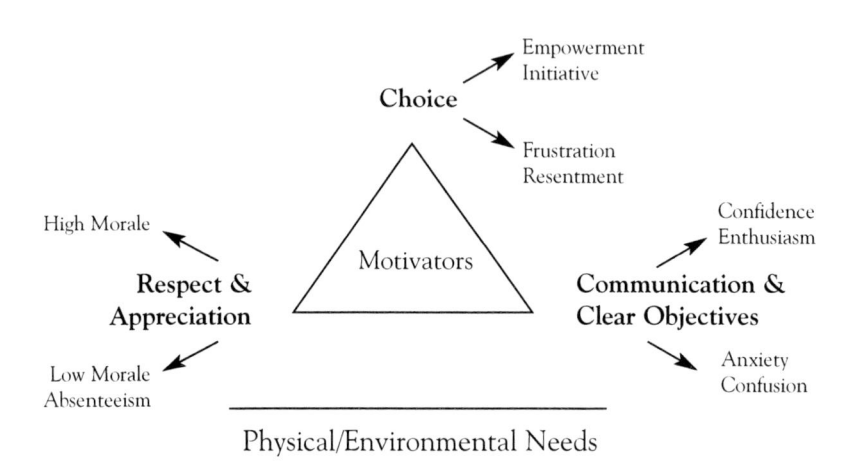

```
                          Empowerment
                          Initiative
              Choice    ↗
                       ↘
                          Frustration
                          Resentment
                                              Confidence
High Morale                                 ↗ Enthusiasm
          ↖    Motivators
  Respect &                    Communication &
  Appreciation                 Clear Objectives
          ↙                                 ↘ Anxiety
Low Morale                                    Confusion
Absenteeism
              Physical/Environmental Needs
```

LOVE, RESPECT & APPRECIATION

The need for love and recognition is critical to our fundamental self-esteem, self-image and sense of personal identity. We depend on these to be able to accept ourselves and develop fulfilling relationships. The stories of Dorothy and Rhiannon illustrate ways in which these human needs can impact on our lives. They are both thirty-something young women. Dorothy is a business consultant expecting her first child and about to go on maternity leave, and Rhiannon is a teacher. First Dorothy comments:

> " 'Love your neighbour as yourself!' People miss the point and they don't love themselves. So many people don't like themselves. People get into relationships that they are not happy in because they couldn't possibly stand being alone."

When our needs are met in the corner of Love, Respect and Appreciation, we experience joy and delight in our personal lives, and high morale in a work context. Of course these can be interchangeable – some people are fortunate enough to feel joy at work, while others admit to enjoying their work.

When our needs are not met in this corner, we feel either extreme feelings of grief and loss or the lesser emotions of disappointment, apathy and low morale or poor self-esteem. Grief is usually associated with bereavement or the break up of a close relationship. But it is not too strong a word for the feeling of loss of identity caused by redundancy, or by the speed of technological progress which materially changes the role required in a job. The lack of motivation that results can lead to actual absenteeism, or being present in body but not in spirit.

UNDERSTANDING, COMMUNICATION & CLEAR OBJECTIVES

The need for understanding is about making sense of our environment and overcoming the fear of the unknown. It concerns learning and teaching, how we communicate and exchange information and how we integrate knowledge, from the big picture to the fine detail. These issues are particularly pressing at times of change in our lives, whether we are facing our first day at school or reorganisation at work.

When things go well in the corner of Understanding or the more job-related area of Communication and Clear Objectives we experience excitement and confidence. We can perform well because we know what is expected of us and we have the information necessary to succeed. This might be in the form of a job description, a street map or a recipe.

All too often however uncertainty abounds, especially in times of 'down-sizing', 'streamlining' or restructuring processes that result in redundancies or require people to re-apply for their own jobs. We grow anxious about the future when information is withheld and the goal posts are continually moved. Unfortunately information is often seen as a form of power in organisations and is used in a manipulative way. One manager may hang on to information because it makes her feel powerful. Another may remain silent because there is no news to pass on and she does not wish to appear ignorant. In terms of meeting the needs of staff however, it is better to *say* that there is no news rather than let rumours spread.

FREEDOM & CHOICE

The territory of Freedom and Choice involves distinguishing between what is within our control and what is beyond it. This boundary needs to be clear and we need to be able to move between those two areas adjusting our behaviour accordingly. We have a right to choice, but that is balanced by an obligation not to abuse the freedom and power that we have. There is a lot to learn in this corner about control and influence, negotiation and the different styles of leadership.

When our Freedom and Choice needs are fulfilled we feel exhilarated and empowered, creative and ready to use our initiative. We feel involved in our destiny. We are able to put an individual stamp on the job we do, even though it may have to comply with policies and directives that are beyond our control.

When we are denied control we feel the powerful emotions of anger, frustration, outrage or indignation. These can be turned out towards others as in aggression and violent behaviour, or inward on the self as in depression. If this is an issue you need to address, you may find Gael Lindenfield's [4] exploration of anger helpful – a practical book full of strategies for managing anger constructively.

Rhiannon, the teacher, experienced the whole range of these manifestations of anger as she struggled to come to terms with the effects of having a father with a volatile temper:

> *"The anger and outrages seem to originate from when I felt frustration at having my needs unmet in my earlier years. This became particularly marked in my teenage years and I found feelings got "locked inside" and then came out with such venom and anger that I would almost lose control and feel like I wanted to really hit something."*

The energy of this corner of the emotional triangle can also be channelled into non-violent protest and activities such as campaigning for causes.

Rhiannon came to find her anger was useful as a force for change, but she found herself always on the edge of being aggressive, never quite in control:

> *"This spewed into my adult life where my sense of justice conflicted with the attitudes of many of the lecturers I encountered. They seemed to mock or judge the people who I considered my peer group, the working class. Hence, I carried the "torch" if they were criticised. My fighting spirit was channelled into "causes" about women's rights or subject battles. Here the passion was for the good, but I found that this could spill over into real anger if I wasn't listened to. I would feel personally rejected, rather than simply professionally disagreed with."*

In some ways Rhiannon's aggression seemed to be a positive advantage:

> *"Some positive factors of the passion and anger was the way that it would help to keep me going, but the constant adrenalin build ups were taking their toll on my health."*

The effect on her physical and mental health eventually brought her to a counsellor after three serious bouts of depression.

Anger is the emotion that most people are afraid of. We tend to experience it differently according to our socialisation. Traditionally little girls have been discouraged from expressing anger, (good girls don't have tantrums), and there is still evidence of this even in 21st century attitudes to bringing up children. Little boys, on the other hand, are 'allowed' to show anger, but it is much less acceptable for them to give way to tears, (big boys don't cry). As a result, many women suppress anger, or we find ourselves shedding hot tears when we are angry because it is the 'only' expression open to us. The tears tend to get interpreted as weakness, which increases our frustration and we are caught in a vicious spiral. Conversely, I have met many men who find themselves unable to express grief and become irritable instead.

Our needs are not, of course, as neat as they are in the diagram: life is not triangular. The needs overlap and emotions mix, sometimes becoming complex and difficult to disentangle. But although the diagram may be over-simplified, it gives us a way in to analyse complex experiences and a language for naming and talking about them. Try applying it to your own emotional life.

> EXERCISE - YOUR MOST IMPORTANT CORNER
>
> Put some time aside – about half an hour. Make the usual preparations as described in Chapter 2.
>
> Draw a version of the Human Needs Triangle and explore each corner in turn.
>
> How do you get your needs met in each corner?
>
> Do you tend to give more or receive more, or is this evenly balanced?
>
> What are the consequences of your needs not being met? How do you tend to behave when this happens? How does it make you feel?
>
> Now decide which is your most important corner. This is the corner of your most fundamental need. If things are OK in that corner, you can cope with your other needs being frustrated.
>
> Finally, note where the gaps are in your needs being met. Think of ways of filling these gaps and write down a plan to achieve this.

EXPRESSING EMOTIONS

This is where we need to get our hands dirty, metaphorically speaking. The housekeeper in a Victorian household was high in the hierarchy of servants. She had her own sitting room, supervised other servants and so on. At the bottom of the hierarchy was the scullery maid who got all the worst mucky jobs to do. If you aspire to the title of 'Emotional Housekeeper' you first have to work an apprenticeship as scullery maid and get to grips with clearing out your emotional dustbin. This bin will be full of all the negative emotions that you haven't expressed in your life.

The so-called negative emotions are not all negative. They are perfectly healthy reactions which only become a problem if they are bottled up. We can easily see what we need to do to be healthy by watching the behaviour of children. For instance, if a normal two year old is frustrated by the necessary rules that parents impose, she or he will have a tantrum. It may be difficult or embarrassing to handle, especially in the middle of the supermarket, but once the feelings are expressed, the child's system returns to normal. A natural process has run its course. Similarly, if we experience bereavement and have the opportunity to grieve fully, expressing all the desolation, fear and anger that will emerge, then we return to being able to function in our lives more quickly than if this process is denied. We may think we can cut it short or avoid it, but if we do, the grief is likely to surface again in later years in the form of physical or psychological illness.

Dorothy recognised that reclaiming her emotional life and her confidence meant becoming to some extent like a child:

> "I think that I've always been quite strong and lived on my emotions. In the early teens, that was successfully suppressed by pressure from other people. It was the realisation that it was OK to be that way, to be expressive, that got me out of a kind of fug. In a way I kind of became a child again. Do you know what I mean? Because children don't have any inhibitions. They don't worry about what people say."

Dorothy was aware that adults were 'not supposed' to express emotion, but refused to be ruled by this expectation and avoided further damage.

Adrian, a local government officer with a consistently calm manner, recognised that continually repressing his anger was having a depressing effect on his life:

> "We are going through restructuring. The control issues are incredible. Power games, lack of information, disregard for people's anxieties. I'm in a situation where to rant and rave should be a normal part of every day. To crash around and break things up and throw things through windows - certain people I think as well - would be a perfectly normal thing to do. But what I do is go around controlled. I meet people who say they also feel so frustrated, and angry about the way people are being de-powered. And with that, wisdom, clarity and all the rest disappear.
>
> "There is something about all this kind of cold bureaucracy that I need to shout and rave about. And I rarely do, and what I lock up with all of that is a lot of joy."

Shortly after this conversation Adrian left his job and set up as an independent management consultant.

Ironically, as Adrian noticed, it is by fully embracing difficult emotions that we prevent them from overwhelming us. When we value them in this way, instead of leaving them to congeal in an emotional dustbin, we can use the energy they contain in our lives.

Beth was a training manager in a small company that was taken over by a multi-national. Until then her flying phobia had not been a serious inconvenience. Now she had to overcome it if she wanted to keep her job. Beth describes how she went about it:

"To do that I had to walk straight into the teeth of the fear. You don't do that alone. I had support and permission, acceptance. You must have someone to be there for you. It was a bit like setting up a controlled explosion I suppose. Then I could fall apart and shake and let the tears flow and it wasn't some embarrassed passenger next to me or a stewardess I didn't know. But I survived and it was a breakthrough. Breakthrough is the word. There was light on the other side and I broke through into elation, exhilaration, like I would never have believed. All that excitement and energy had been locked up in my phobia."

Beth went on to become a frequent flier and delighted in the opportunities this opened up for her.

Learning to set up and manage this kind of 'controlled explosion' is part of becoming emotionally competent.

EMOTIONAL COMPETENCE

Emotional competence is one of the skills of emotional intelligence. Senior managers in business are increasingly recognising that they need this quality in their teams. They need it every bit as much as technical skill and intellectual brilliance if they are to succeed in today's marketplace with its rapid rate of change. Studies of companies worldwide as described by Daniel Goleman[5], showed that emotional intelligence was in fact rated twice as important as technical competence in recruiting new staff.

Emotional competence as described here is based on the ideas of John Heron[6] and Denis Postle[7]. It is based on the principles of co-counselling, a method of self-development which is a particularly effective tool in learning to understand and manage emotions.[8] Emotional competence is about awareness, expression, communication, and control of your own emotions, and acceptance of other people's emotions.

To be emotionally competent you need to be able to:

1. Get to know your own emotions
2. Empty your emotional dustbin
3. Tell people how you feel, calmly and without blame
4. Switch off your emotions when necessary
5. Accept other people being emotional around you

The last three abilities depend upon the all-important second skill: emptying your personal emotional dustbin. Without this, the other skills are not achievable in the long term.

1. GET TO KNOW YOUR OWN EMOTIONS

The first step is to learn to distinguish between emotions. Notice how an emotion makes itself felt in terms of body signals and sensations. For instance, we may yawn, shiver or have stomach gripes when we are frightened, or feel a boiling sensation inside if we are angry. Everyone is different and it's worth taking some time to identify your personal signals. They will not only be different for each emotion, but will also differ in intensity according to the occasion. For example, yawning can signal avoidance or mild anxiety, whereas sweating and stomach pains may accompany more intense fear when a situation cannot be avoided.

EXERCISE – GETTING TO KNOW YOUR EMOTIONS

Put aside half an hour. Make the usual preparations.

Take some time now to check through each emotion – grief, sadness, fear, anxiety, anger, frustration. Identify how you recognise them.

> What are the internal triggers you notice in yourself?
>
> What are the signs that other people might be aware of?
>
> Now follow the same process for each of the positive emotions of joy, excitement and independence. These get neglected because they don't cause us a problem. But consider, do you notice when you are happy? Do other people know?
>
> The next stage of becoming familiar with your emotions is to understand where strong emotions come from, what triggers them and why. We are then less likely to allow emotions from the past to influence current relationships inappropriately. For example, if a colleague or neighbour reminds us of a former schoolteacher who bullied us, we may experience fear or dislike of this person without realising why. Rather than acting inappropriately on those emotions from the past, we do better to recognise and deal with them without taking them out on our innocent colleague.

2. EMPTY YOUR EMOTIONAL DUSTBIN

It is important to distinguish between expressing and communicating emotions. Expressing them involves being emotional, while communication is a calm and rational activity. We tend to avoid expressing emotions because it can get us into trouble or because we are afraid that, once started, we will be unable to stop. But not expressing them is far more dangerous. Not expressing emotions is like treating them as rubbish. The more we throw away, the fuller our emotional dustbin becomes, until we are using all our energy to keep the lid on it. Then one more, often trivial incident upsets us, we explode inside and the lid comes flying off. Emotional debris scatters all over our nearest and dearest and other innocent bystanders.

DUSTBIN THEORY
Traditional Models

Beth, the training manager, reflects on different ways of emptying the dustbin:

> "I've heard people say they can transcend all that old emotional rubbish, meditate it away for example. I'm not sure about that. Maybe they can. Everyone is different. But for me it means going into the pain and going through it. That's the only way I get free of it.
>
> "Otherwise whatever is bugging you drags you down. You think you'll drown in the tears, or you won't survive a fear, or that if you get angry you'll hurt someone. So you put the lid on it all. And that's where your energy goes, keeping the lid on. But the worst thing is, you are never strong enough. The lid flies off and that's really messy. You hurt people who have nothing to do with it all. And that leaves you feeling guilty on top of everything else. Best to go for the controlled explosion."

Quite apart from the damage done to our relationships by this kind of fall-out, repressing emotions on a long term basis can seriously damage health, as discussed in Chapter 7 - Body Knowing.

Dorothy was clear that failure to empty her dustbin had made her ill:

> "I have quite a few experiences of that, where it has actually made me ill, when I was in my late teens, early twenties. It came out as depression, real depression, so much so that I had to see the doctor. On occasions I was put on anti-depressants to try and overcome it when really, thinking about it now, what I needed was **somebody** to help me overcome it. But I guess the GP didn't have the time and my parents certainly didn't have the capacity to understand."

Full expression of emotions is a cathartic or purging process requiring a safe place and a witness who is willing, prepared and skilled in allowing and/or facilitating the catharsis. We can do this with a suitably qualified counsellor or therapist. It is better not done with family or friends, as however hard we try, it is hard to keep personal issues out of such a process.

I believe that most people who have the lid tied down on a full dustbin need several such sessions to lift the lid and begin the process of clearing. It is by far the most effective way of shifting the build-up of rubbish and freeing the tension and energy that is involved in holding emotions inside. What is more, it is usual for an emotional purge to be accompanied by insight into stubborn behaviour patterns. There will be an "Aha!" which allows us to re-evaluate the way we live our lives and to move forward in new ways. Some people may need to continue in this way for some time. But this is not a question of 'not being able to stop'. This needs to be a structured process with a purposeful contract and sessions planned at regular intervals.

Having done some clearance work, most people are ready to move on to a maintenance regime, maybe using a journal, meditation or a physical method of keeping energy moving. It is always possible to return to the cathartic process in difficult circumstances, or if the dustbin fills up.

> EXERCISE – EMPTYING YOUR DUSTBIN
>
> Put some time aside – at least half an hour, preferably an hour. Make the usual preparations.
>
> Consider the following questions:
>
> What methods do you use to empty your dustbin and/or keep it empty?
>
> Are they sufficient and effective? What are the consequences of not emptying it?
>
> What do you need to do in addition?
>
> What steps do you need to take to achieve this?

3. TELL PEOPLE HOW YOU FEEL

Communicating about emotions is very different from emotional expression. Compare these two scenarios:

Your boss has made a decision that upsets you. You smash your fist on the table, shout and swear and storm out of the room, slamming the door behind you. You are too upset to work, the row has repercussions on the whole team and you can't sleep at night. Next day it takes more time to repair the damage with your boss and restore reasonable working relations. You are also aware that it will affect your appraisal.

In the second scene your boss announces the same decision. You walk to the window and take a few moments to breathe deeply and compose yourself. Then you turn round and calmly but firmly make the statement, "I am very angry about this." The two of you then go on to have a difficult but constructive discussion about the reasons for your anger.

There is a world of difference between actual loss of temper and making a calm but vehement statement. The second opens up the possibility of discussion, while loss of temper muddies the water and gives the other person the chance to refuse to communicate further.

It is important to recognise that communicating calmly about emotions is almost impossible if your dustbin is full. Sooner or later the backlog of negative emotion will leak out in tone of voice, body language or a sarcastic parting shot. If you fear that this will happen, leave the scene of the argument. Come back later (after a dustbin emptying session) to make your communication. It is perfectly legitimate to do this after a few hours or even the next day, and is preferable to risking a full-scale row.

4. SWITCH OFF YOUR EMOTIONS AS NECESSARY

Sometimes it is necessary to set aside both negative and positive feelings in such a way that there is no emotional leakage. This may happen when personal issues are overwhelming but there is a need to do a professional job. Equally we may choose not to intrude with our good news on the grief of a friend, or to mar a celebration by expressing anxieties. And sometimes we judge that contributing our own emotions would simply inflame a situation.

The danger here is that we shut our emotions down and then forget to return to them. A number of habits encourage this. We may have been taught that emotions are not important and that we should not let the heart rule the head. We may believe that our own feelings are less important than other people's. Or we may be 'too busy'.

It is vital however that we do revisit the emotions we have switched off, or the dustbin will start to refill and the neglected feelings will come back to haunt us. We risk losing the balance between the professional and personal and living a life of compartments. We may feel cheated of our feelings of joy and excitement and resentful of our friend's grief. Never be too busy to attend to this crucial aspect of emotional housekeeping.

5. ACCEPT OTHER PEOPLE BEING EMOTIONAL

We often feel embarrassed when others express emotions. This comes partly from lack of experience of what to do to help, and partly from a fear that our own emotions might escape. Learning the skills of both expressing and controlling our own emotions makes this much easier to handle. We can relax about our own emotions, and the practice of emotional housekeeping will also have taught us what is likely to work in witnessing and accepting other people's emotions.

An extra dimension of this principle is necessary to people who hold the roles of manager, team leader, supervisor, mentor, therapist or facilitator. In addition to tolerating the emotions of others, they will find it invaluable to learn the skill of helping others to express their emotions. The first steps are listening and acceptance. Those who need more sophisticated skills may learn them on a counselling course.

Dorothy feels strongly that learning to be emotionally competent has developed her sense of self at work and made her a more confident person in relationships and in her family:

> "I think I'm more a master of my emotions. If I need to preserve my sanity basically I walk away from a situation. For example the last job that I left. If I hadn't done that, I would have allowed them to get me into the same situation again. So I just walked away. Some would say that's giving up. I would say no, I needed to live, to have a sane existence. I don't see the point of coming out at the end of something

and saying, 'well I stuck with it, I saw it through to the end. And actually you're mentally scarred by it! So I can do that now. You've got to go your own way. You've got to live inside your own head and therefore you will know what is best for you, and you will find the means to make good."

What would your Wise Woman do?

She would open her heart and let her tears flow.

Then she would know what to do.

58 - THE WISE WOMAN WITHIN

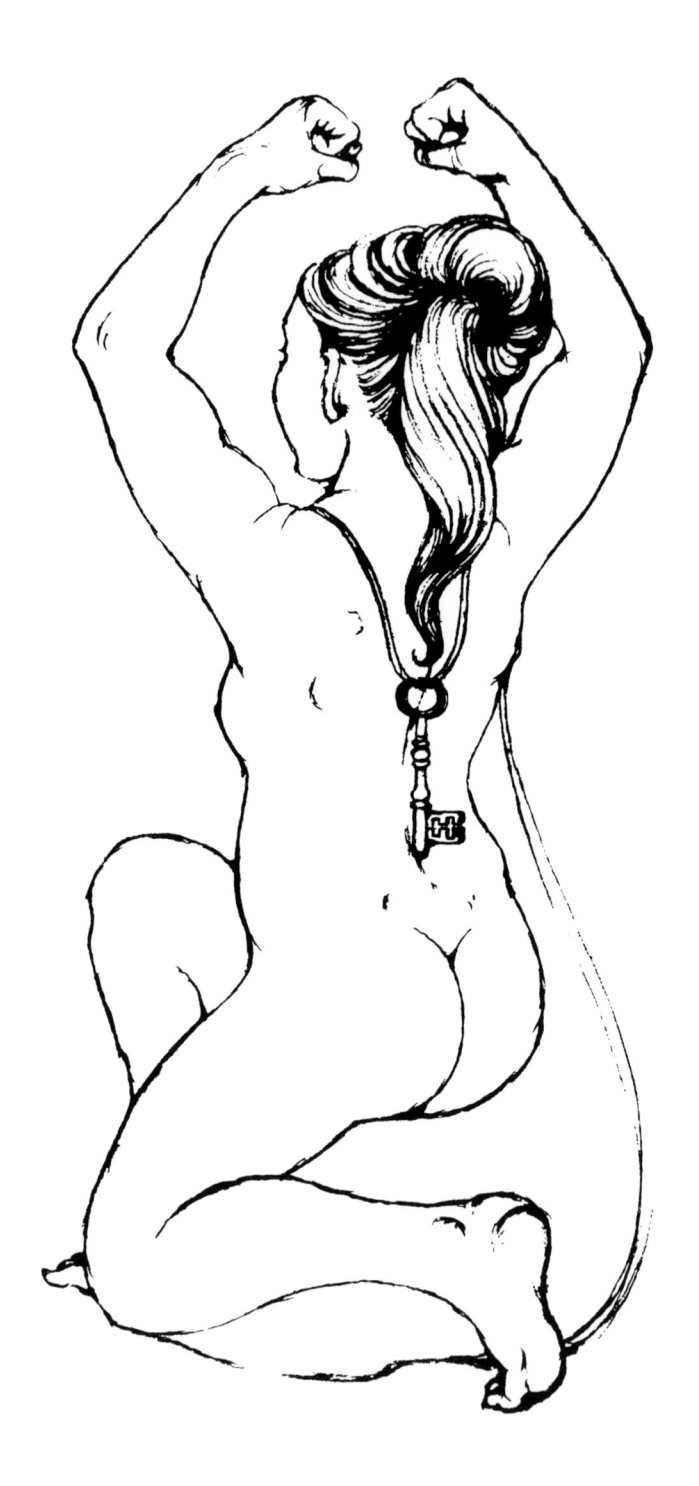

– CHAPTER 4 –

DEVELOPING PERSONAL POWER

"Anger is energy – our personal jet fuel. It is telling us that something needs adjustment in our lives."
Christiane Northrup[1]

How do we turn anger into jet fuel? We know that emotions can stop us being confident and assertive. They get in the way. We hold back for fear that our tears will let us down, or that we will come across as too abrasive. But now we have learnt to empty the emotional dustbin, all that can change. We are ready to move on and use the newly released energy to develop personal power.

It is all very well to be confident on an assertiveness course. It is another matter trying to achieve it within the family or at work. Transferring a new skill is always challenging, especially if conditions are unfavourable and it feels as if the world is against you. When you first address emotions in an unfamiliar context you will probably feel shaky and may not express yourself as clearly as you planned. Like anything else, this needs practice. Be purposeful. Make a plan and try it out in a relatively unthreatening situation to build your confidence.

It helps to have a structure like the one below which I developed for checking out situations that felt charged, involving either individuals or groups. It applies, either fully or in part, to most contexts whether personal or professional, and works well alongside the Human Needs Triangle. It has often helped me to stay centred in the midst of difficult conditions. The mnemonic SWIG seemed appropriate because it usually made it less likely that I needed a stiff drink at the end of the day! I could take a swig of clarity and insight instead. Next time you have a problem with an individual or group, try going through these steps.

SWIG

SELF	Is the problem in me or out there?
	Manage own feelings, suppress paranoia and prejudice.
	Use intuition. What does my gut say?
	Check out past influences. Who does this person remind me of?
WHY	Why is this happening?
	Is there a practical reason for the problem? Ask about circumstances.
	Apply Human Needs Triangle - Love, Understanding, and Freedom.
	Consult, discuss, with colleague as sounding board.
INTERACT	Show interest, ask questions, listen to their story, meet the real person.
	Draw attention to, raise awareness of their behaviour with them.
	Invite mutual problem-solving, negotiate assertively.
GROUP	Make a 'here and now' comment about group or family energy.
	Balance needs of individual/group.
	Invite group to share decision making in context of ground rules.
	Use the group's support — 'group-ally'.
	If someone leaves, check and acknowledge group feelings.

SELF

Look first at your own attitudes and your perceptions of what is going on. This counters any tendency to put the blame onto other people.

Check for paranoia! Lack of confidence can sometimes produce paranoid imaginings that other people are being hostile. This was the recurring hurdle I had to get over in my early days of facilitating groups. Solving it requires that you stoke up your self-esteem.

We sometimes project past problems onto situations in the present so make sure you aren't jumping to unfair conclusions about someone you hardly know. A structure for dealing with this situation is described in the next chapter.

WHY

Next ask yourself why this is happening. There may be a good reason for someone's preoccupation or grim expression. Maybe they have a train to catch, an ill child, stomach pains. Or maybe you have failed to appreciate a good piece of work, or you have withheld the information they need to write a report or make sense of an instruction. Mentally check out which of their human needs may be unfulfilled, and how you might remedy that.

INTERACT

The obvious way to find out is to ask them. You may prefer to avoid someone who is making you uncomfortable, but remember, going to meet the problem is usually the way to find the answer. Why prolong the agony when the explanation may be simple and the solution within your power? You may be surprised at the person and the attitudes you find when you get talking and discover that your assumptions are unfounded.

GROUP

If you are uncomfortable in a group, team or family situation, it is worth commenting on how the energy of the group is feeling to you. Someone else may feel the same way. At least it is a way of opening up the discussion without being personal. Exploring why these feelings have arisen may well lead to talking about people's behaviour and working out a compromise about how it may be changed or tolerated.

Growing personal power makes it possible to negotiate in this way without apologising or becoming aggressive. This is a kind of 'power-within', which is very different from the 'power-over' that is oppressive and imposes its will on others. Personal power-within has strength and confidence that enables us without disabling others. We experience it inside the self as a sense of quiet inner authority and certainty. In relating to others it allows us to be open and intuitive without threatening others, feeling threatened by them or becoming paranoid. It involves being alert and listening, while remaining sure in the knowledge of what we are doing and why we are doing it. We can be convincing, grounded and relaxed when expressing our point of view with no aggressive insistence that the other person should give up their position.

MANAGING CHANGE

Change causes many people to lose touch with their personal power, especially when it is uninvited. It is a time when we need it most – in order to appraise the situation calmly, to pursue the answers to our questions and to assess what resources we need to face the challenge. Usually the turbulence of change rocks the boat of human needs and so the Triangle from the last chapter is a useful framework for analysing the opportunities and dangers involved.

Sara Glennie, a friend and colleague who is a change consultant, was working with social workers in local authority children's services at a time of local government reorganisation. She used the Human Needs Triangle as a tool in deepening her own and the workers' understanding of their predicament. They were experiencing profound disorientation, disillusionment and depression. Many seemed to have lost any belief in their professional competence and most were having difficulty seeing a way forward. Sara was well aware that at times of change people need information about how things will be different, and consultation about how change will be implemented. But she also recognised that they need to maintain awareness of what will stay the same. Efforts to introduce change will therefore be more effective if there is a simultaneous focus on behaviours that promote stability.

For instance, consider the bottom left of the Triangle. If a manager continues to recognise and value the achievements of staff, they will maintain their professional self-esteem. For, although structures and job titles may be changing, this does not negate the skills, wisdom and experience that make up professional identity. The watchword here is "don't forget what you know!" It continues to have value. Focus on how to transfer it and apply it in the new context. Failure to recognise the continuing value of professional knowledge leaves people feeling de-skilled and disillusioned. It undermines morale, demotivates staff and leads to depression. The baby of professional expertise gets thrown out with the bath water of change and, and to mix metaphors, much time is subsequently spent re-inventing wheels.

Moving across to the bottom right hand side of the Triangle we see how critical communication is at such times. Managers who are leading their staff through change need to be aware of just how slowly many people absorb and adjust to the news of change. If rushed, they may dig their heels in simply to buy time. This can spark a chain of reactions that take managers and staff further and further apart. Once this happens, opposition can become a matter of principle, even if the only thing wrong with the new ideas is that they are new. If on the other hand, staff are given space and answers to questions, they are less likely to close their minds.

People's need for information becomes urgent and insatiable at times of change. It is the manager's job to keep communication channels flowing. This maintains interest and enthusiasm and stimulates questions, curiosity and ideas. If a manager becomes defensive and fails to communicate, people are thrown into confusion, mistrust and suspicion. Fear of the unknown, including the threat of job loss can become paralysing.

At the apex of the Triangle, managers introducing change have the opportunity to motivate their staff by inviting their participation. Flexible leadership is critical here. On the one hand, managers need to state clearly what is non-negotiable, so that people understand their boundaries. On the other hand, they need to use facilitative skills to promote engagement with the choices that are available. Consulting staff about how best to introduce necessary changes generates creativity, ownership of the process and commitment to it. The danger is that managers' own fears may lead them to take control and be prescriptive, which risks breeding resentment, resistance and sabotage.

MANAGING EMOTIONS IN A WORK CONTEXT

There is still resistance to acknowledging the contribution of emotional intelligence to the commercial bottom line. Some organisations or managers are still buying into a philosophy best expressed by the motto "when the going gets tough, the tough get going". This attitude labels anything that addresses emotions as touchy-feely or wimpish. This is odd when we consider the power of emotions. Think of the creativity strangled by fear, the constructive working relationships destroyed in boardroom rows and the staff who leave because their achievements are not recognised. Think too, of the passion, compassion and indignation that have motivated some of the great artists, inventors and reformers. These so-called wimpish emotions move mountains. The 'tough guys' are happy enough to use emotions to bully or manipulate others. But they take fast evasive action when it comes to facing their own emotions or respecting those of others.

Enid was a transformation consultant in a multi-national company who challenged this cultural taboo on emotions head-on:

"My purpose is to find a legitimate place for tears in the workplace. The tough guys are at one end of the spectrum and here I am with my tears at the other end. Of course there are times when the tough guys have to get going and lay it on the line. But there are also times when emotional expression is acceptable.

"In complex systems there's a place for a whole range of skills and different types of people. The secret – and that goes for people and for systems – lies in achieving a balance of skills and choosing the right ones for the job in hand."

Enid was a highly competent, creative and confident woman, and she readily shed tears in supervision sessions with her manager when she felt strongly about the issues under discussion:

"I have no problem with this, I look forward to a time when people will regularly get together and express their emotions, and it won't be California.

"But I do realise that I have to take responsibility for the image I project when I cry. It's like I have to renegotiate the meaning of my tears. Otherwise people continue to be embarrassed and then they discredit me. So I discussed it with my manager and we were able to create a context for tears. I would say something like: 'I'm upset. That doesn't mean you have to look after me. I am not trying to manipulate you. The fact that I feel strongly is relevant to the issue but there's no need to feel uncomfortable about it'."

I wish that I could have introduced Enid to Pierre and listened to their discussion of this issue. Pierre was a manager who found himself in a minority of three men among many women managers on an assertiveness course. He lived for his work and held very traditional views:

"All women who cry are using their tears to manipulate the situation. They turn up in my office and as soon as they see they are not going to get their way, they turn on the waterworks."

Once the very vocal indignation had subsided, a worthwhile exploration of both points of view took place. Pierre, the two other men in the group, and the women were able to discuss the misconceptions and mistrust involved and to move toward a better understanding for the future.

Establishing trust is critical to managing complex situations, often involving change, which generate strong emotions. You need strong foundations for this work and the keystone is being able to trust yourself, as Enid did. To achieve that, you need to understand yourself and to love yourself. It's back to self-esteem!

A TEAM ACKNOWLEDGING THE EMOTIONAL DIMENSION

At this point it is worth recounting the story of a five-day teambuilding event, which I facilitated with a colleague and which engaged with emotions at a number of levels. Like Enid, the team progressed to setting a context for emotions which contrasted strongly with the culture of the organisation in which they worked. The team in question worked a 3 shift system to provide 24 hour technical support in a leading software company. In many ways the week could be described as an intensive course in emotional competence. Nearly all team members learnt a great deal about some or all of the five principles described in the last chapter.

The process of change started some weeks before the course. The team manager thought he was a good manager and well-liked, but this was not the whole story. It was therefore important that he committed to, and was prepared for, some tough feedback from team members. He made the commitment lightly, confident of his popularity, and as the week unfolded showed impressive courage in sticking with it, learning to listen and to really hear the unwelcome truths that were presented to him.

The course included two outdoors sessions, on the Tuesday and Thursday respectively, so that there was time to both prepare for and debrief this work. Two outdoors facilitators ran these sessions in some woods where the set-up included a high and a low ropes course and a number of ground level structures and activities. All the activities planned were based on co-operation or personal challenge rather than on competition. We hoped that difficult communication lessons might be learned more readily in the woods and that the metaphors would transfer to the indoor setting. The outdoor work would also engage the large number of young team members who would be bored indoors. All these hopes were fully realised.

A critical part of the process was getting group members to surface their fears. This happened in two stages:

On the first evening people wrote up their worst fantasies about the coming week. They were then helped to turn these into positive statements about what they hoped would happen. For instance, several people expressed a fear of heights in the context of work in the woods. One of these converted into: "I am moving safely and confidently several feet above the ground." These powerful incentives were posted up on the wall to act as signposts and beacons for the days to follow.

The second stage of surfacing less obvious fears emerged while debriefing the first of the two outdoor sessions. A number of fearless young men had exhausted the challenge of the high ropes, and were planning to use the equipment blindfold, and to do activities backwards in order to 'up the ante'. When encouraged to explore what would be really challenging to them, they all admitted that facing emotions would be harder than facing physical challenge in high places.

Several were then prepared to put the competitive ego aside, and made it their challenge to address a different kind of fear, and to provide support for a frightened person attempting to conquer their fear of heights.

For this to work, the frightened people had to be prepared to trust the very people they had least inclination to trust, that is, those who least understood their fear. These also 'happened' to be those whom they found most difficult to work alongside. Once the risk of admitting those fears had been taken, handling the next stage of co-operation was relatively easy. When the young men got close enough to the fear to see how genuine it was, they no longer felt tempted to mock, tease or criticise. They had no time to feel embarrassed because they were absorbed in working out how to offer support in a way that was practical but not intrusive. They were delighted to discover in themselves the capacity to be sensitive, and relieved that it was OK to be gentle. Their fearful partners were equally relieved to find it OK to be frightened and were grateful for the help in overcoming their fears. The self-esteem of the fearful people rose as their fear was met with unquestioning acceptance, good humour and patience.

This development allowed the young men to show their gentle and caring side, which in turn led not only to breakthroughs in relationships within the team, but to a shift in the team culture. People were relieved to move away from a culture of scoring points or making jokes at other people's expense. In the new culture people could confront each other's behaviour without triggering a defensive reaction, and gradually a new habit of openness, co-operation and support was established. As a result, long-standing relationship difficulties involving several team members were addressed and healed.

The course was remarkable both for the range and degree of emotional competence learned, and for the practical outcomes. It showed me beyond doubt that people of all ages and both genders are capable of a phenomenal response when treated as whole human beings. They responded with tireless energy to grow trust and confidence, take risks, rise to challenges, and build working relationships capable of solving deep-seated problems with long-lasting results. I was fortunate that continuing work in the company brought the opportunity for ongoing contact with team members. They reported that the effects of the week were still developing eighteen months to two years later.

It is worth trying the Affirmation Technique with one of your own fears. The rules are that the emerging statement must be:

1. In the first person. It's no good making affirmations for other people. Don't expect "my son is tidying his room" to work.

2. Positive. This means eliminating words like 'fearless', 'without', 'not' and 'loss'. Find ways of focusing on what you will gain.

3. In the present continuous tense. "I am swimming" pushes you to believe in the reality, whereas "I will be able to swim" keeps the possibility forever in the future.

4. Emotionally charged. Your Affirmation should feel challenging, although not to the point of being totally unimaginable.

You can find ways of drawing these affirming statements to your attention, as we did on the team-building event by displaying them on the walls. Try writing them out every morning or sticking them on your mirror and in other places around the house.

> ### EXERCISE – MANAGING EMOTIONS IN RELATIONSHIP
>
> Put some time aside – at least half an hour, preferably an hour. Make the usual preparations.
>
> Take some time to consider whether there is a relationship in your life where you are holding back feelings. Is this suppressing a part of you that could be of practical value in helping the relationship forward?
>
> How risky would it be to be more open?
>
> What is your desired outcome?
>
> What support would you need and where can you find that support?
>
> How can you prepare?
>
> What is the worst thing that might happen? How likely is that to happen? Can you handle that?
>
> Reflecting in this way often gives a new perspective on a situation. Do not however, take any risks without support, without a positive purpose, or if you feel unable to handle the consequences of not meeting acceptance. As the team members found, it is more important to be gentle with yourself and to go at your own pace than to be competitive and intrepid.

What would your Wise Woman do?

She would remind herself of her skills and experience.

Then she would know what to do.

72 - THE WISE WOMAN WITHIN

– CHAPTER 5 –

OUR PARENTS OURSELVES

"Blame is useless. Blaming gives away power. Keep your power. Without power we cannot make changes."
Louise Hay[1]

A sure way to upset many people is to say "you're so like your father" or "you're just like your mother". They tend to react with indignation, nervous laughter or denial. These protests are by no means limited to those who had unhappy or abusive childhoods. We find them among people who have a good relationship with their parents. This is partly because we all want to be individuals in our own right, but mostly it is because at some point in our childhood a vulnerable part of us was deeply offended by a piece of parental behaviour.

This hurt tends to live on in our Child's responses to people in adult life whose appearance or behaviour reminds us (usually unconsciously) of that particular parental behaviour. Other authority figures can also be involved, with bullying teachers high on the list of people who can leave these lasting emotional scars.

Have you ever felt angry with a stranger for no apparent reason? Do you have a colleague you find hard to like even though he or she is popular with everyone else? If so, it may be that these people subtly resemble someone from the past like your Maths teacher or a parent. If that happens once in a blue moon, it doesn't really matter. If however, you find yourself coming close to tears whenever you are asked to add up figures, or mistrusting all men with beards, then it is worth doing some detective work aimed at solving the problem.

So we need to separate the person we encounter in the present from the baggage we carry from the past. In order to do that we must take a closer look at the baggage. It may be an uncomfortable process but there is immense value to be gained in this exploration. We can trace how we have become what we are, and we can learn to understand the relevance of the past to our current situation. If we understand our personal history we can take responsibility for our self, both for what we inherit and for how we choose to develop that self. This is best illustrated by returning to Jan's story of her childhood introduced in Chapter 2. You will remember that she was living in a cosy world where it was no problem to gain her mother's approval by being good.

> "As I grew up, Dad was around more but he thought I was a feeble creature. I couldn't catch a ball or do Maths and I wouldn't say boo to a goose. He laughed at me and tried to goad me into having an ounce of initiative. Of course I could always run and hide in mother's cocoon, but that had come to feel pretty stifling, definitely a last resort.

> "I almost wished I'd been a boy but I was terrified of boys. They were always chasing me and torturing me at school. School was a nightmare because I'd almost never met another child before I was left there on the first day.

> "It was really hard pleasing Dad. He was always out there in the garden doing something dirty and cold, and I was supposed to be 'in the warm' with mother doing something domestic. Mother always assumed I was on her side. They didn't have rows but there was always an undercurrent of nagging or criticism. She used to say things to me to ridicule whatever Dad was doing. I guess that was really unfair but it didn't occur to me at the time. It just used to make me feel hot. I used to want to be on his side of the triangle but then I would feel guilty of deserting mother. She made me an accomplice against silly men."

Jan later worked out that she had been caught in a trap of being punished by her father and rewarded by her mother for doing, or not doing, the same thing. He would have said he was trying to encourage her to be different when he laughed at her clumsiness and her fear.

While her mother laughed in quite another way, to reward her, making a virtue out of her incompetence. In fact her mother persuaded her to pull back from succeeding, because success was a betrayal of 'us' who were unathletic, a-political, unintelligent, women.

> "Dad had a typical stance when he was in the garden and he'd escaped from some sludgy stuff going on indoors. He'd stand like a statue as if he had taken root in the vegetable garden. He'd keep his back to the house and you could pretty well see his bad temper radiating towards you.
>
> "One day I remember I was actually outside playing! And I was suddenly confronted by the statue from the other side. I'd made a kind of den behind the shed and I was in there, not hiding exactly but just being in my own world. And then it was all spoilt. The statue arrived and planted itself right in line with my hiding place. I had to stay absolutely still and silent, so that he wouldn't know I was there even though he seemed to be looking right at me. What I saw was deep sulk! The corners of his mouth pulled in with irritation, slitty eyes. All so familiar. I felt engulfed in sulphurous fumes, invaded. But I couldn't escape. He'd have been so embarrassed, angry. So I froze for what seemed like forever until eventually he moved away."

Jan grew up but her Child never moved on, at least not until she 'saw' herself decades later. She stayed frozen in that moment, constantly watching, and never proactive. This rabbit in the headlights pattern was to limit her in future years when other male figures would take the place of the father statue gazing on her hiding place, exhibiting signs of anger and exasperation in no way directed at his hidden child. Her Child would nevertheless feel threatened, and the woman would mysteriously falter and lose touch with her truth, her world.

EXERCISE - MEETING THE REAL PERSON

Put half an hour aside. Make the usual preparations.

If you regularly feel uncomfortable with someone for no reason you can think of, try using this process to find out why. It is good to do this with a partner who can ask you questions, but you can also use your journal.

1. First describe the person in fine physical detail.

2. Next identify anyone that the person reminds you of, or who comes to mind as you go through your description. If you draw a blank, take each item of the description and write down people you have known in the past who, for example, had blue eyes, or wore glasses, or used a particular gesture or walked with a limp.

3. State exactly what these two people have in common and then explore what was difficult about your relationship with the person from the past.

4. What do you want to say to this person? What feelings need to be expressed? Do whatever is necessary to deal, in your mind, with any unfinished business.

5. Now identify how the person in the present differs from the person in the past. State the person's name and make a clear distinction between the two people. For example: "You are Mary, my next door neighbour, not Miss Potts who used to teach me geography."

This process should help you to see "Mary" more clearly as a person in her own right. It does not of course guarantee that you and Mary will be good friends, but it may give you a better perspective on the difficulties between you. For example, you may need to ask Mary to turn her radio down at night, but you do not need to vent on her all the anger you feel towards Miss Potts for humiliating you in geography classes.

MAKING SENSE OF THE PAST

The story that Jan tells is not an unusual one. Although the individual variations may be infinite, similar themes are recognisable in the stories of many people. This was a child with loving and well-intentioned parents who provided her with a stable home and a good education. Neither child nor adults were ever considered to be anything other than 'normal' and reasonably 'well adjusted'. At any point in her story things could have taken a turn for the worse, but they didn't.

The story illustrates how complications can arise out of ordinary circumstances. Certainly we should be grateful for a relatively trouble free and happy childhood, but each child's experience of that childhood is unique. However lucky we may have been, it is still valid and useful to trace adult difficulties back to their roots in a so-called normal upbringing. Some people prefer not to, but others find this necessary before they can accept it and move on.

Let us be clear that we are not setting out to blame the parents here. What we are dealing with when we explore the past in this way is our *perception* of what went on in our families. It is not possible to give an account of 'how it was'. That is too elusive a concept to capture. What we remember of our parents are *descriptions* of *memories* of childhood, experiences viewed through an adult lens, which will shift like the patterns in a kaleidoscope as we look back over the years. They are probably as much fantasy as fact, although the experiences were nevertheless formative. The 'once upon a time' framework is therefore very appropriate to such memories.

This takes us a long way from the temptation of wanting to blame our parents for all our faults (whilst retaining the credit for our qualities!). Equally, the remembered difficulties are not the fault of the child. As children we do not have power and do not carry responsibility for what happens in our lives. Generally speaking, there are no rights or wrongs, there is no blame to be apportioned, just people doing the best they can. There are at least four reasons for not blaming our parents:

1. Because of the love and/or respect we may have for them

2. Because we honour their life experiences which made them how they are

3. Because, as adults, we know how impossible it is to 'get it right' in the role of parent, having either had experience of that role or known close friends or family with children

4. Because we want to grow up and take responsibility for our own lives. If we claim that our behaviour patterns or self-image are the fault of our parents, then that leaves us believing that these habits are still in their control. This belief locks us into the victim position. Alternatively, if we accept a piece of behaviour without judgement as simply our response to their behaviour at that time, then we can own it, let go of it, and move on

I must emphasise that the argument described above does not apply to anyone who has experienced abuse during childhood. Abusing parents are not doing the best they can, or if they are, then their best does not amount to good enough parenting. In those circumstances, anger and outrage are appropriate responses, and very necessary to the process of leaving the past behind and building a new future.

The novelist Nuala O'Faolain has her heroine, Kathleen de Burca, reflect on the effect of having the security of mother love on the development of a child. She is watching a child learning to walk:

> *"The mother stands behind the child ... and he knows that there is a mass of love behind and above him ... That must be what gives the healthy people the gift of unself-consciousness. ... They are themselves through and through. The shelter of love made them honest."* [2]

Kathleen is struggling with the effects of the emotional neglect she suffered as a child. Although her mother's abuse of her children was not deliberate, Kathleen nevertheless experiences it as a handicap in adult life. Later it occurs to her that maybe her own mother was raised in an institution, *"one of those brutal orphanages ... where they whipped you if you wet your cot"*. If that were so it would explain *"why she didn't know that mothers are supposed to love their children."* Kathleen chooses not to pursue that thought and gives herself the counsel, *"do the best you can."*

You may find it difficult to be introspective. There are always those among friends or family who tell us it is unnecessary or even dangerous to explore in this way. Equally insistent is the inner critic that accuses us of self-indulgence. It is sometimes unpleasant to poke about in the garbage of our emotional life, and we may have a resistant or lazy part that fights quite hard to make us give up.

In addition women are often expected to suppress their pain along with their creativity and their whole inner spiritual process. We need instead to acknowledge it, understand it and use it. It is no accident that our emotional garbage pile tends to be constructed against the door to our spiritual world. The irony is that it both blocks the path and acts as a rich compost, all of which makes the exploration worthwhile. We need to recognise how rich it is, this so-called garbage, and not reject it. It reminds me of a Wishing Tree I stumbled across in Cornwall with my husband. It stood to one side of a muddy track leading to a sacred well. Every branch was thickly festooned with 'wishes' represented by ribbons and rags of every kind including strips torn from supermarket bags and 'J' cloths. It was a moving sight, being such a mixture of the sacred and the profane and evidence of ordinary people's belief in the power of the spirits of that place.

If we are to endure and justify the sifting of garbage, we need to be clear about why we are doing it, what difference we want to make. One aim may be to find a link between the world of inner experience and the outer world of action, a balance between reflecting and doing.

There is no point in spending a lot of time working on ourselves, if we do not also spend time using the energy and insight gained to be more effective in our lives. Introspection among the dark and mysterious roots of our being needs to be balanced by moving out into the sunlight and making a difference in the world. I have often been amazed at the vision and sense of direction that can come from digging around in those roots, and getting a clear understanding of their knotted and twisted shapes. However oddly contorted they are, they still can produce strong branches, beautiful flowers and nourishing fruit, and it is no coincidence that our deepest roots connect to the furthest-reaching branches.

Try applying this analogy to an activity in your life. I suggest that you choose an area that is causing you to reflect. Maybe it is very demanding, or you feel you are getting nowhere, or you are wondering if it is worth the effort.

EXERCISE - ROOT AND BRANCH

Put some time aside – about half an hour, longer if you can. Make the usual preparations.

Imagine that you are a tree, with your roots spreading down into the earth of the past out of which you grew as a seedling. Your branches are stretching up into your future.

To explore the balance between your own root and branch activities, apply the following series of questions to the area of your life you have chosen:

1. On the practical, tangible, everyday level ask yourself:
"For what reason am I doing this?"

Frame your answer "Because ..." with a glance to past difficulties.

For example: "Because I lose confidence if I am challenged/because I find women with varnished nails/men in suits threatening/because I'm afraid of the dark."

> 2. On the same practical level, ask yourself: "To what end do I do it?" "What are the outcomes?"
>
> Reply in terms of the results you hope for.
>
> For example: "With the result that I am becoming more confident/less aggressive."
>
> 3. Tune in to the inner dimension, asking "What is my purpose in this?"
>
> To which you might reply: "I do this in order to let go of the past."
>
> Then pursue this question further: "Is this enough? Do I have another purpose?"
>
> And then you might reply: "I do this in order to transcend the past/to realise a vision/to find my life path/to make a difference."

UNPACKING THE BAGGAGE

Until we recognise and understand the patterns that we carry with us from childhood they will continue to have a hold over us. This is illustrated by Dorothy and Rhiannon's comments on their upbringing in similar cities. Dorothy begins:

"Both my parents were very, very passive.

"I started thinking about the upbringing that I'd had, that my parents had been, not discouraging but not encouraging either. They were typical dockyard city, the service culture - know your place and a high degree of duty, that kind of thing. Not suppressed, but it wasn't right and proper to "show off" I guess. So therefore if you had any confidence in yourself, it was pushed out of you. So any get up and go that I had myself was kind of quashed.

"My mother is very timid: She will not say anything that could possibly cause what she would see as an argument. In other words, she won't

express an opinion in a group of people because she's afraid that somebody might express an opposite opinion. You end up talking about trivia."

Caught between this role model and her own strong personality, Dorothy found herself *"wanting to explode inside"* whenever she wanted to express an opinion herself.

In Rhiannon's family there was more expression of opinions but this made it no easier for her. Rhiannon experienced similar feelings and often exploded on the outside as well. She held a position of middle manager in a secondary school. When she suffered her third serious bout of depression she started to examine her aggression:

"I found myself crying for the least little thing. The aggressive behaviour was directed at anyone - the kids I taught who I saw as lazy, and staff who "got away" with doing the minimum. I ruled very strictly, biting heads off for wrong uniform, make-up, jewellery, lack of homework etc.

"I was Rhiannon the teacher, a woman who was successful and had beaten the odds - fighting in most things I did. For example, Dad said it was a waste of time me going to college as I would just get married and have kids. He threatened not to sign my papers. So my behaviours certainly came from home. Mum was pretty passive, although she worked hard, but never had any time for me unless she wanted me to do something. She told me once that I could always be a prostitute if all else failed. Mum and Dad were always arguing and I could see my husband and I repeating this."

Rhiannon began to see that her problems stemmed from her childhood experience. She was repeating patterns of family behaviour at work and in her marriage. Once these patterns had helped her survive but now they were undermining her:

"My Mum said something that triggered a significant "aha" moment. She said that I had to be noisy to get a word in edgeways at home and

> *the only way to get space or to get my siblings off my back, and my parents, for that matter, was to blow my top. Then I would be temporarily listened to. This behaviour became repeated at work as I related to school in a family way, never aware of how they were separate.*

> *"As the eldest of 5 children I was always in charge of the others, copping it if they misbehaved and hating life at home because of the chores. My solace was in my studies, and I never really felt valued - picked on by parents and siblings, unless they were parading me off because of my boobs or the fact that I went to grammar school. Dad had a volatile temper and so I inherited and copied a lot of that."*

Both Dorothy and Rhiannon escaped from home into relationships that intensified their problems. Dorothy had a series of partnerships where she felt "half of a whole". Now however, she is married to a man who was a friend first and a lover second. She operates as a whole person with him and is determined to raise their child to be confident in himself.

Rhiannon left her husband and had eighteen months off work with a slipped disc. In this way her body gave her the space for reflection on her life and her identity:

> *"The final dawning ... I realised that I was a pleasant person and began to like myself. Now I am more at peace with myself and can therefore be a more tolerant person. I enjoy more of my life and have been able to forgive much of what happened in my childhood."*

Some women realise that their father has provided a more positive role model than their mother, which may have resulted in giving them more confidence in the world.

Lesley is a successful complementary therapist and educator. She feels passionately about her work and strives to establish complementary medicine as part of the whole healthcare picture, and to work in collaboration with mainstream practitioners. She lacked an acceptable role model in her mother and instead chose ways of being that felt more male.

> *"I think my personality was shaped more by my father than by my mother. I learnt to make things happen and can be quite fierce. I always wanted to be different and individual and I took that from my Dad. I led quite a double life when I was a teenager, I was a real rebel."*

It is quite possible to recognise that an inheritance has been a strong influence in your life without resentment or even regret, and it is refreshing to encounter this.

Hayley took an Open University science degree as a mature student and had a keen interest in environmental issues, but she had first made a career as an air stewardess:

> *"What really triggered me into becoming an air stewardess was my mother's frustrated desire to see the world. She transmitted a love of travel to me and I was travelling for her as much as for me, always sending postcards wherever I went. Being an only child I was the only one who could fulfil those dreams for her. I don't regret it, but if it had been otherwise I might have become a scientist."*

Most parents set out to give their children the best possible chance in life. How they define that is determined by their own experience both as children and as adults. There will be things they want to repeat and things they want to avoid and they will have differing degrees of success or failure. Their children will often not share their definition of success or failure. Their different perspectives and the comfort of have someone to blame often leads to a misinterpretation of 'mistakes' that are made.

For example, I saw my education as deficient because I emerged with little confidence or understanding of life. My parents however viewed it as a success because I did well academically. What I resented however, was that they had given me a choice of schools which had not been honoured. They asked, *"do you want to go to school x or school y?"* I chose school x, but they sent me to school y. When my father discovered how upset I had been over Christmas dinner some thirty years later, he was genuinely sorry. His opinion of each school had been so strong that he couldn't believe I had meant what I said. *"That headmistress at school x was so wishy-washy about discipline,"* he protested. But I had seen her as someone who wasn't afraid to let her pupils develop their own personalities. Visiting her school, I had felt welcomed and believed I could flourish in the creative atmosphere. By contrast, the headmistress at the school I eventually attended had seemed cold and afraid to be herself or to treat children as human beings. I never had reason to review that first impression. When I discussed this with my father all those years later, I felt listened to for the first time. Similarly, I saw his point of view, which had not occurred to me before. We reached an understanding and the betrayal I had felt was healed.

At this point it may be helpful to undertake some analysis of your own inheritance. However, delving into relationships with parents can be unexpectedly powerful. Material may be uncovered that it is difficult to cope with alone. I have therefore chosen not to include a formal exercise for doing this. If you know or suspect that you have difficult issues in this area that need addressing, I suggest you find an accredited counsellor or therapist to work with you.

If you are confident that you can cope with such an exploration, you might like to take the Human Needs Triangle of Love, Understanding and Freedom that you used earlier, and go through it with either or both of your parents in mind. How were their needs for love and recognition met? How did they manage communication and make sense of the world? How constrained or independent were they, and how did they manage boundaries? How does their map of needs compare with your own? How do you imagine all this influenced their ability to meet your needs? These reflections may give you new insights into why your parents behaved as they did. If it throws you into unforeseen turmoil, consider obtaining the help of an accredited counsellor or therapist.

What would your Wise Woman do?

She would examine the past for its messages.

Then she would know what to do.

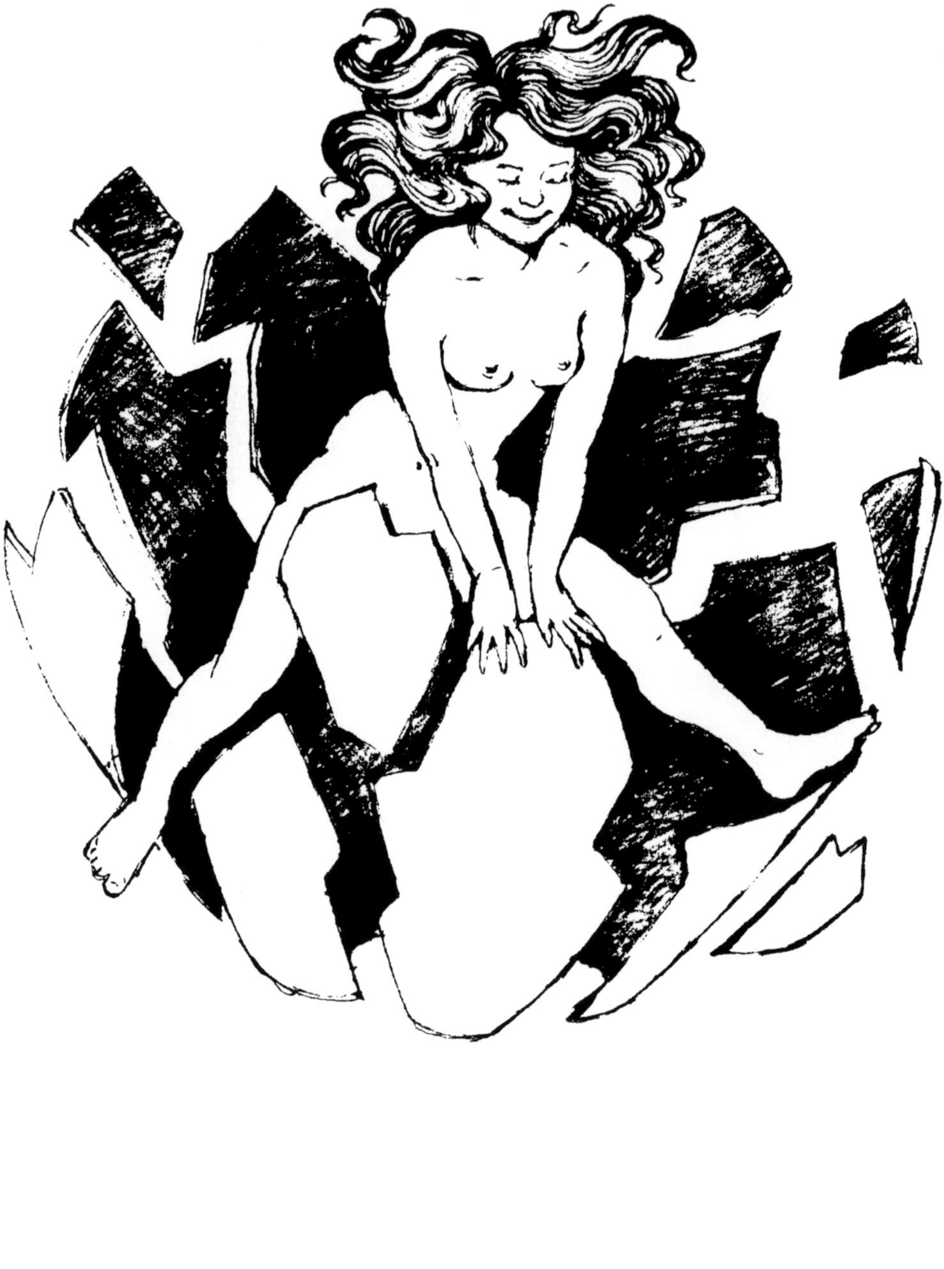

– CHAPTER 6 –

BREAKING THE MOULD

*"Whatever the problem is, it comes from a thought pattern,
and **thought patterns can be changed**.
"Remember: **you are the only person who thinks in your mind!**"*
Louise Hay[1]

What effect does your inheritance have on your current behaviour? Do you find yourself following the same patterns that you developed as a child? Or do you tend to do the opposite, sometimes more for the sake of it than because it is helpful to you now? Alternatively, you may combine a mixture of the two, like Rhiannon who rejected her mother's passivity but copied her father's aggression. Is it time to break the mould of this conditioning?

Our behaviours tend to revolve around our fundamental needs for freedom and independence and for love and nurture. This is the dynamic that is played out in families as children obey parents in order to win their love and approval. It is a pattern we tend to repeat in adult relationships. So there are clusters of behaviours that show us negotiating boundaries, asserting or surrendering independence, using or abusing power and leading or being led; as well as clusters of behaviours that are about giving, receiving, withholding and refusing love and recognition.

What we want from our parents is that they conform to the all-loving, all-wise archetype of the Mother Goddess and Father God. Whether or not they are wise and loving, they are all-powerful to the child and they often continue to be psychologically powerful long after we have grown to physical independence and left home. Archetypes represent human behaviours expanded and writ large, and they appear in all cultures in their myths and fairy tales and legends. For example, the Father God holds the power in the form of Thor, the Norse thunderer and Jove, Jupiter and Zeus. The Mother is represented by the big-breasted earth goddesses of early civilisations, by Demeter, Ceres and Kali the all-nurturing, all-devouring mother goddesses.

Sometimes we put parents, mentors and lovers on a pedestal, seeing only their admirable qualities, so that they seem like gods or goddesses. In the same way we stereotype people negatively – politicians, students, lager louts – refusing to entertain that they too may have more to them than the bad news that hits the headlines. It is more comfortable to have the ideal to look up to and the demon to blame than to admit we all share the same capacity for admirable and despicable behaviour.

Putting people into pigeonholes stops us seeing the whole person. The danger is that we fall into the trap of assuming there is no more to a person than the label on the box. However, it can be useful to adopt shorthand descriptions about *behaviours* in order to understand why we do what we do.

Stereotypes are the much reduced, human scale reflections of the behaviours depicted in archetypes. Human lives are messier than those of the gods. Our needs all run into one another. They overlap, interweave and conflict. We can't always cope with the complexity, so we resort to stereotyping to cut through the confusion, often focusing on faults and magnifying them.

These faults can usually be seen as overdone strengths. This is a useful concept both for understanding the behaviours better and for finding a way toward forgiveness. It is also invaluable in situations where giving constructive feedback is appropriate. People are better able to 'hear' feedback about their shortcomings if they are framed in this way. For example, if you tell someone, 'this report is far too detailed. I can't see the wood for the trees,' they are likely to find the criticism hard to take because it is wholly negative and devalues a key skill. Try instead something along these lines: 'Your eye for detail makes a vital contribution to the quality of our service, you don't let anything slip through. But in some contexts it becomes an overdone strength. This report is for senior managers, they don't have time for detail. Far better to show the big picture more clearly and not confuse the issues.'

SOME MASCULINE & FEMININE STEREOTYPES

As we have already noticed in Jan's story, aspects of behaviours in men we encounter in adult life may well remind us of our fathers, or of other important male figures in our childhood. If we found those behaviours difficult as children, and were powerless to do anything about it, then meeting the behaviours as adults is likely to trigger a childish response and we will feel trapped. It will therefore be helpful to prepare for meeting these stereotypes with more confidence.

In women, behaviours may remind us of our mothers or they may mirror our own behaviours that we have internalised, sometimes unconsciously, by copying our Mother role models. It is often said that it is our own faults, seen in others, that irritate us most. This may be why. It is useful to identify our own internal 'saboteurs', those parts of the self that tend to pull the rug from under our feet when we most need to be confident and balanced.

THE MOTHER FIGURE

A number of stereotypes come under the heading of Mother Figures. One is the Wicked Stepmother, straight out of the fairy tales and equally relevant to modern life, whether as a 'real' stepmother in a family, or someone who has stepped into the shoes of a favourite manager. To explore this stereotype, let us drop the 'wicked' label and examine what it might feel like to be in the position of 'stepmother'. She might feel uncertain and insecure; oversensitive to criticism; an intruder or a usurper of someone else's role; fearful and inexperienced; reluctant to take on the role; resentful and jealous of existing relationships.

And what about the 'stepchild'? This may be a 'real' child in a family, or it may be the Child inside an adult. She may also feel uncertain and insecure; frightened, hurt and vulnerable; deserted and betrayed; jealous and guilty because she fears that it may be all her fault. The previous mother figure is elevated onto a pedestal of blameless perfection. The stepmother is a perfect potential scapegoat for all ills. Small wonder that the stereotype exists, but lifting the label gives us a better chance of seeing past it to the person behind.

The Mother Hen is the original smother mother who wraps the people she sees as her charges in cotton wool and fusses over everyone she comes across, convinced that only her constant interventions can make them comfortable or safe. The idea that life is not worth living without an element of risk is foreign to her. She constantly warns to be careful and throws a wet blanket over any proposal that is exciting or daring.

Office Mother women may be of any age, with a friendly approachable manner and an ability to put anyone at their ease. At best they are noted for their diplomacy and willingness to listen. If these qualities are exaggerated we find mother hens who make a fuss of male bosses, encourage an over cosy atmosphere and stifle initiative. They will too readily take on the role of rescuer and prevent people from learning from their mistakes. Good Office Mothers, on the other hand, can uphold the emotional agenda of the workplace in a way that feels 'natural' and acceptable because they are women. If they can do this assertively, without taunting or patronising men, they can be valuable role models of good people managers.

THE NICE GIRL

Whereas Mother Figures find it gratifying to nurture others, the Nice Girl group of stereotypes seek to gain approval to boost their self-esteem. The Nice Girl wants to please everyone and will accommodate to anyone's wishes in order to be liked. Nice Girls tend to fall victim to Bully stereotypes, who may be male or female. Those who play the Nice Girl role include many, many women – from dowdy or glamorous mature women to naïve or sophisticated young girls.

Sophie was an interesting combination. She matched the Nice Girl stereotype whilst also filling the role of Office Mother as part of her job as a senior secretary:

> *"I would remind my boss discretely of the personal things going on in the lives of his staff when he needed to know. Birthdays, kids being ill, death in the family, rocky relationships, that sort of thing. I also found myself acting as counsellor, offering a listening ear to people almost twice my age. I actually gained a lot of satisfaction from knowing that they went away better able to concentrate on doing a good job of work. My own needs always came last, and I would stay late to complete work. I'd make excuses for my boss, because it was nearly always his bad planning that made it necessary for me to stay on."*

As time went on, however, Sophie realised that her job was simply an extension of her Nice Girl personality, the little girl that grew up pleasing her mother:

> *"I was brought up to be a good little girl and be quiet and do what Mummy says. You know, don't be outspoken and all the rest of it. And maybe it sounds silly, but when you're a secretary, that's an in-that-mould type job."*

Soon after gaining this awareness, Sophie applied for a programming job and started a new career.

THE BULLY

Masculine stereotypes often involve the use or abuse of power because traditionally, in many cultures, power has been associated with the male role in the shape of the benevolent ruler or the tyrannical dictator. These give rise to the negative stereotype of the Bully. Other stereotypes are driven by a combination of power and love needs. For example, the Woman-Hater may appear either as the Womaniser or the Wife-Beater. The Womaniser appears to love women, seeking endlessly for the unconditional mother-love he never had, but always contriving to have his revenge indirectly in adult relationships with women. The Wife-beater's outbursts of physical or verbal abuse are often followed by expressions of remorse and promises never to repeat the abuse, which are not kept.

On the other side of the coin of the Bully type is the Hen-pecked Husband, who anxiously defers to others and tends to fuss about ineffectually attempting to please. The story of Terence illustrates the potential relationship between these two opposite stereotypes.

As a manager in a large organisation, Terence was a kind of Bully. He was not physically or verbally abusive. He did not slam doors or call people names. He was cold, unapproachable and task-focused. He paid minimal lip service to the personal development plans of his staff, never expressed appreciation for good work and never admitted to being wrong. Terence did not discuss work issues with his team but made arbitrary decisions about who should do what. Once his mind was made up he was impervious to the reasoned arguments and creative ideas of his highly competent staff. This behaviour and his solid build earned him the nickname 'the Tank'.

I met Terence and his secretary, Julia, separately at first. Then they both came on a Managers and Secretaries course, which was when this story emerged.

One weekend Julia had reason to call at Terence's house with some papers. As she stood on the doorstep she heard a woman's voice shouting and listened to the following exchange:

"Terence! I thought you were going to get these windows cleaned this morning!"

"Yes dear, just as soon as I've finished loading the dishwasher and clearing up in here."

"And you haven't forgotten the lawn?"

"No, dear."

"Before it rains!"

As Terence opened the door in his apron, his wife swept past him to her car, calling various other instructions over her shoulder. Julia felt highly embarrassed but Terence simply shrugged and commented that his wife had a stressful job. He made coffee, thanked Julia profusely for the extra work she had done for him and invited her to see his porcelain collection. Julia described how, in the quiet of his study in front of the displays of colourful pot lids, Terence was a different man:

> "I wouldn't know a pot lid from a yogurt pot, but he just came alive. He told me all about them, and all the time he was stroking them gently with his big fat fingers. He described the piece he most wanted to find as if it was the perfect woman and he just couldn't wait to fall in love with it at some time in the future."

The next time Julia saw Terence at work she thought she saw a flicker of amusement in his eyes as they met.

> "He never mentioned it. I didn't expect him to and I never said anything. But he always seemed more civil to me after that. But then again it might just have been that I wasn't afraid of him any more. It's difficult to know whether it was him or me, but something changed certainly."

What changed was that Julia stopped seeing Terence as a stereotype, having witnessed something of the whole person. And Terence, having been 'rumbled', was able to bring a little more of himself to work. He had thought this would undermine his authority, but found it had the opposite effect.

THE DOORMAT

The Downtrodden Doormat is the feminine equivalent of the hen-pecked husband. She is a Nice Girl who has deferred to others for so long that she hardly knows who she is. The Doormats tend to be shy, retiring and lacking in confidence. Like Dorothy's mother, they are self-effacing and motivated by the need to avoid conflict. They have an inability to say no, low self-esteem and difficulty knowing their own mind. When you ask them what they want to drink and they reply, "whatever you're having", it is partly because they don't want to be any trouble, and partly because they really don't know what they want. They are often to be found at the photocopier on a Friday evening when everyone else has gone home or to the pub.

THE CRITIC

In contrast to the Nice Girls are a group I call the Critics who seem to thrive on making difficulties for others. They are convinced that they are right and have a need for control. The Fishwife is the most strident and storms in to trample over everyone else's needs and sensitivities. She is never wrong, jumps hastily to conclusions and is quick to judge, blame and criticise. She is the feminine manifestation of the aggressive bully. The Nag and the Nitpicker have much in common with the Fishwife, but go about their interfering ways more quietly and less directly. They are the constant drip that wears away the stone, but will wear a look of injured indignation if a hen-pecked partner suddenly explodes in anger at their carping.

THE MARTYR

A more complex stereotype is the Martyr, who is really a Fishwife disguised as a Doormat. She seems to set out to get her own way, but refuses to be direct and also makes sure that she fails. In spite of her constant complaints she is resistant to any change that might improve her position. For Martyrs enjoy having something to complain about. Their game is to trigger guilt in others in order to get help without having to ask for it directly. Help will always be rejected because no-one can be trusted to do the job as well as they can. They exercise power through manipulation.

Evelyn was a personal assistant to a budget holder within a University. I met her on an assertiveness course I ran when she was in conflict with her boss:

> "My boss really enjoys working with spreadsheets, but that is supposed to be part of my job. I don't mind that because I find them tedious. The trouble is though, that then he's too busy to fulfil his other responsibilities. And he delegates them to me. I'm flattered that he trusts me with these tasks, but I actually don't have the skills or the authority to complete them. I'm not trained to do those things and I really resent the fact that I'm not being paid to do this level of work."

Evelyn complained bitterly about this situation on the course but was resistant to changing it. She was encouraged to clarify her job description, to refuse inappropriate work and to take the matter higher if necessary. For every suggestion made, she produced a reason why it wouldn't work, and refused to entertain the possibility that she had a way out of the situation.

THE AVOIDER

Another group of stereotypes are best described as Avoiders. They may appear variously as the Joker, the Tease or the Hair-splitter.

Whatever their disguise, Avoiders use it to mask themselves and their feelings. In avoiding showing their beliefs, concerns and vulnerabilities to the world they also avoid any depth in encounters with others. When others attempt to develop a theme, they keep the conversation at a superficial level by side-stepping with a joke. The Tease constructs relationships on the premise that people enjoy being teased, all the time, about every aspect of their appearance or behaviour. Anyone who doesn't co-operate is further teased for being a spoilsport. The Tease expects to be teased back, but only so far. As soon as remarks come too near the bone, the aggression that is behind the teasing begins to appear. The Hair-splitter keeps interaction at a similarly trivial level but takes a more intellectual approach, being pedantic about grammar and the meaning of words and insisting that people say precisely what they mean. He (or she) can avoid the point of a discussion indefinitely and persuade others that he has won an argument, without once engaging with the spirit of the matter in hand.

You may find these stereotypes in men that you meet, in parts of yourself or in other women. These stereotypes are by no means exhaustive, so it may be useful to spend some time adding those you have noticed yourself. Note the ones you find most difficult to handle and reflect on what you do when you encounter people who fall into that grouping. There follows an account of how one woman explored her difficulty with a powerful man whose behaviour in meetings matched the stereotype of the Bully.

THE STORY OF A WOMAN DEVELOPING HER POWER

Veronica, a senior woman manager in a University, was struggling with her fear of a male colleague, a fellow Dean on the senior management team. Her fear was so strong that it was preventing her from contributing to meetings where he was present. It was not appropriate or necessary to explore whether this problem had its origins in a relationship with a father figure, although there were some clues that this might have been the case.

"I can't be in the same room without my gut churning. I just feel physically nauseous. It's completely disabling.

"I don't want to confront him directly even if I thought I could ever do that. I have to rule that out because I think it's too risky. It would almost certainly make matters worse. The bottom line is that I have to be able to work with this man and the other members of the management team. I need to approach this whole thing indirectly. Maybe I could use a combination of the techniques you've suggested."

First she worked alone on a mental exercise involving the colleague.[2] In this she visualised him on a stage and chose both pleasant and unpleasant things to happen to him. She found it necessary to have her 'revenge' by dowsing him in icy water, before she could achieve the symbolic forgiveness of giving him a pleasant experience. This process allowed her to see her colleague as a whole human being rather than simply her tormentor, a vital shift of perception.

Secondly she gave attention to her body language and voice projection. Veronica had a habit of listening with arms crossed, shoulders slightly hunched, head down and eyes intent on the speaker in an attitude of rapt attention. This unassuming air was effective in meetings with her own faculty staff where she aimed for peer discussion and mutual co-operation. However, in situations where she needed to display confidence and an air of authority, this attitude gave an impression of little-girl submissiveness. We therefore focused on straightening her posture and gaze, which also opened her throat and airways allowing easier voice projection. A colleague then worked with her on some voice exercises that further helped her delivery.

Finally Veronica planned a strategy for her next meeting with the 'difficult Dean'. Putting time aside to prepare and rehearse was uncharacteristic behaviour for Veronica, who was used to thinking on her feet in her busy schedule. Part of the plan was for her to initiate a conversation on her own terms before his presence could start to undermine her confidence.

The effect of this combined approach was dramatic. She managed her fear well enough to contribute to meetings, to win this colleague's respect and to initiate a project with him that enhanced the working relationship between their two faculties. She was then able to extend the strategy to other situations. At a luncheon to welcome the new Chancellor she made such an impact that she monopolised his attention, to the evident frustration of male colleagues, including the Dean who had once intimidated her.

It is important to note three things about this process. The first is that Veronica only chose methods she felt comfortable with, and also altered them to suit her purposes. Not every technique suits everybody. The second point is that she worked on her own perceptions and behaviour and did not demand that her colleague change. Lastly, she did not end up being great friends with her colleague.

> "He's changed how he is with me completely. He actually seems to have developed some respect for me. But that doesn't mean I like him. I don't like his arrogance and his chauvinism. That's all still there, but my attitude to it has changed. I accept that he's just like that, and nothing I do can change it. But now I can look past it and work with him. I don't let that influence the way I act. And I don't let it affect the way I feel about myself."

The process that Veronica started here did not only benefit her working life. She took up meditation at about this time and soon afterwards experienced a kind of vision that gave her a strong sense of herself:

> "I was driving along and I suddenly saw a bright white, dancing figure in my mind's eye very clearly. A very strong feeling came over me that it was OK now to let 'me' come out into the world. It was almost like a child whom I had been protecting for a long time could now be exposed to the real world, but with care. It has made me feel much stronger inside and more aware of myself as an entity apart from a role at work. I feel much calmer and in control."

These experiences also seemed to affect Veronica's relationships. She had an unexpected meeting with her father soon after this and was able to talk more openly than she ever had before. He was pleased to get to know what sort of person his daughter was, and she was able to *"appreciate the man behind the father figure."* It seems that, by refusing to be bullied, rejecting the victim role and yet avoiding being aggressive herself, Veronica opened up a pathway for the emergence of her own inner self. This gentle, but nevertheless powerful part of herself would probably not have considered it safe to emerge if Veronica had chosen a more confrontational approach in tackling the relationship with her colleague.

EXERCISE – FACING THE STEREOTYPE

Find a quiet space and time and make the usual preparations.

1. From your list of stereotypes identify those you find difficult to respond to – because they trigger emotions of anger or fear, and/or you lose your own confidence or sense of direction when you encounter them.

2. Pick one of these – the one that would make most difference to your life if you were able to respond to it in a new way. Now give your imagination free rein and jot down as many different ways of reacting in that situation as you can conjure up. Allow yourself to be ridiculous and outrageous. If you are stuck, think of someone who is very different from yourself (maybe much older or much younger, or male if you are female) and imagine how they might react.

3. Select one of these responses – the one that is most likely to be effective in the situation you find yourself in.

> 4. Undertake a risk assessment. Analyse any risks that may be involved and weigh them against the benefits of a good outcome. Don't feel that you are copping out if you decide not to go ahead after this analysis. It is better to start with a simpler situation and build your confidence gradually. Start again and choose a less challenging stereotype.
>
> 5. When you do decide to go ahead, develop your approach in detail. Write down what you will do and say (and possibly wear) and rehearse it out loud. Even better, practise it with an understanding friend. Get your friend to think of the unexpected and things that might go wrong and work out together how best to handle them. Prepare carefully on the day (in body, mind and spirit) and then just go ahead and do it.
>
> 6. Afterwards congratulate yourself on your courage. Write down what went well. What do you wish you had done differently? How differently? Be gentle with yourself. Ask yourself: is the situation resolved? If yes, well done. Let it go and move on. If not, you may want to revisit it. Or you may decide that would be a waste of your energy, in which case feel pleased that you tried, let it go and move on.

THE INTENTION TO FORGIVE

Most parents want to do their best for their children, and most children appreciate them for their efforts – eventually. We may begin by thinking that our parents can do no wrong, progress to blaming them for everything and then arrive at a position where we see that reality lies somewhere in between. We come to understand their good intentions, forgive their shortcomings and appreciate their qualities. The process is part of growing up.

Forgiving is difficult. It cannot be achieved through an act of will. However much you say you want to forgive, if there is some part of you still bearing a grudge, then forgiveness will not happen. If that is the case, accept that you cannot forgive. Accept that you are angry. It is perfectly OK to be unforgiving. It is perfectly OK to be angry.

There are two main things that get in the way of being able to forgive. In the first place there is resistance to fully admitting the extent of your negative feelings. Secondly there is the inability to forgive yourself. It's worth trying a number of different approaches to allow both of these processes to take place. It may not be your style to rant and rage with a counsellor, so try talking it through quietly or have a go at writing about your feelings as a story. Or practice meditation with this in mind. Avoid worrying the subject to death, but aim to revisit it lightly whenever it seems relevant. If you hold the intention to change, eventually something will shift inside you, and what seemed impossible before will happen with no effort.

The exercise below is one way to approach the process of healing your relationship with the people who parented you.

EXERCISE – MEETING A PARENT FIGURE

Find a quiet space and time and make the usual preparations.

1. Visit a place where you feel peaceful and at home. You can either do this physically or in your imagination.

2. In your imagination, bring one of your parents into the space with you.

3. Express any negative feelings you have towards this parent without censorship. Tell them about the ways in which they hurt you, whether or not they intended to do so. Be honest and don't make up emotions you think you ought to have.

> 4. Ask them what it was like for them to parent you and what influenced them from their childhood. Listen to their response.
>
> 5. Thank them for their positive intentions and express all the positive emotions that you have for this parent. Again, be honest and don't make up emotions you think you ought to have.
>
> 6. Say goodbye and write up your feelings and insights.
>
> 7. Repeat the exercise for the other parent
>
> You can meet your parents in this way whenever you like and as often as you like. There is absolutely no need to communicate with your actual parents about this process in order for it to be effective. Although this can occasionally be successful in deepening a relationship, a positive outcome is by no means certain.

What would your Wise Woman do?

She'd make plans, find support and leap into the unknown.

Then she would find she can fly.

106 - THE WISE WOMAN WITHIN

– CHAPTER 7 –

BODY KNOWING

"Be open to the messages and mysteries of your body and its symptoms. Be eager to listen and slow to judge. What you learn may have the capacity to save your life."
Christiane Northrup[1]

Or put another way:

"There is something in my stomach that knows everything. And that's what magic is."
Christopher Corthay[2], aged 6

The physical link with our parents provided one of our first ways of knowing. We gathered our first knowledge of the world in our body cells while still in the womb, laying it down for our future use when we come of age.

What is 'body knowing'? How do our bodies know? And how can we learn to tune in to the messages our bodies send? These are difficult questions to answer because this kind of understanding is, by definition, non-verbal. In response to the question "how do you know?" women will often instinctively clutch their bellies. Occasionally hands fly to cover the heart area. Sometimes we say "I can't explain it, I just know" which can be frustrating for those who only trust more concrete forms of knowledge. "Women's intuition" they will say, dismissing our efforts to be clear. But what is that elusive and notorious thing called intuition? It is actually based on more concrete evidence than is commonly thought.

INTUITION

Intuition is made up partly of experience and partly of sensual responses. The experience is like a database of evidence – cues associated with behaviours – that we build consciously or unconsciously over the years. When we come across a cue it triggers a memory of associated behaviours that we use in making a judgement. Imagine, for example, a child who twirls her hair whenever she tells a lie. A teacher will quickly come to associate hair-twirling with attempts at deception. Whenever she sees the behaviour she will probe further to uncover the truth. She will gain a reputation for having an uncanny nose for lies. If she is aware of what prompts her judgement, she will put it down to experience and observation. If not, it will be called intuition.

But that cannot be the whole story. For children who have no experience of the world often make remarkably sound judgements about people on first acquaintance. They sense when someone is not trustworthy. Maybe they are less easily diverted by words and read body language more accurately. Maybe they pick up contradictions between what is being said and non-verbal cues. Maybe they smell fear in the same way as animals do. Whatever the process, their instincts are usually sound and children are encouraged to trust those intuitions as part of the 'Keep Safe' programme that supports parents and children in schools. If something 'feels wrong' to a child or they get a creepy feel about a person, they should stay well away and tell a trusted adult. I believe that we store these memories and take them into adulthood, which is why intuition seems to live in the belly and why we call it 'gut feel'.

But that is still not the whole story. There is another level of knowledge that is 'laid down' in body tissue as a record of emotionally charged events that happen. As the neuroscientist and researcher Candace Pert writes, *"The body is the unconscious mind! Repressed traumas caused by overwhelming emotion can be stored in a body part, thereafter affecting our ability to feel that part or even move it."* [3]

AN EXPERIENCE OF SURFACING BODY KNOWING

If I ever needed proof that the body knows in this very tangible way, receiving treatment from a cranio-sacral osteopath convinced me. Cranio-sacral osteopathy works to release these effects and restore the rhythm of the cerebrospinal fluid. If we are unable to release the physical or psychological trauma of events, the system tends to contract defensively. This may cause problems years later. These memories, held in body tissue, can date back to a fall last week, an incident in childhood, the process of being born or even to previous lives.

> *"The body remembers, the bones remember, the joints remember …*
> *Memory is lodged in pictures and feelings in the cells themselves …*
> *Like a sponge filled with water, anywhere the flesh is pressed, …*
> *a memory may flow out in a stream."* [4]

On the first occasion I experienced cranio-sacral osteopathy I was mystified. I had recently moved house away from a trusted osteopath and put my back out. I resorted to the 'Yellow Pages' and hobbled in to the local osteopath's consulting rooms. The first surprise was that he treated me fully clothed, the second that there was no painful manipulation. He held my head for a long time, which would have felt very peaceful if I hadn't been wondering when he was going to get started. "He didn't do anything," I complained to my husband on the way out. "But do you feel better?" he asked. That was the third surprise. My back was freed up and I was walking normally!

I later embarked on a longer programme of cranio-sacral osteopathy. The medical establishment had referred me to a dermatologist for a condition I was convinced had a more fundamental cause. The dermatologist's interest was only skin deep in a very literal sense. She declared that she never asked the question *"why?"* as this only led to confusion. At this point I sought help from a cranio-sacral osteopath and started a journey into successive layers of understanding of personal history held in the body. The first layer involved a recent tumble and a more serious fall at three years old. I learnt how the memory of a fall might be held in body tissue, so that the system continues to repeat that falling movement. In counteracting this tendency, we use considerable compensatory energy to keep ourselves upright, eventually become too tired, fall again and reinforce the tendency. The osteopath is able to bring an awareness of this dysfunction to the system. This allows the body's natural intelligence to correct the imbalance and return the system to a state of equilibrium, a change that can be detected. This subtle, non-intrusive 'intervention' resembles the light touch of an elegant facilitator. I was struck each time by the gentleness of the treatment and by the contrasting power of its effect. I would leave feeling peaceful and then experience strong reactions over the following 24 hours. I might be emotional, experience extremes of temperature or become suddenly tired and sleep very deeply.

During further treatment a second layer of understanding emerged, surfacing waves of emotion associated with unresolved childhood traumas. They were accompanied by clear images of people and incidents where I had unfinished business. Although I was usually able to link physical cues to actual events this was not always the case. The release happens regardless of whether the conscious mind understands the links. Images may also appear to the therapist, which may or may not be recognised as relevant to the person being treated. I found the process extraordinary. As the osteopath worked, vivid visual memories or sudden powerful emotions were triggered, just as if he had pressed the action replay button on a video of some episode in my life. The therapist suggested that, far from being extraordinary, this was very ordinary for the body and was a state of business as usual. He did however admit that the way that his hands worked to bring release and balance in the body was to some extent mysterious.

Later I had treatment on the bones of the face and a third stage of my journey back in time began. The work seemed to confirm that the sinusitis experienced since childhood had its roots in the physical trauma sustained at birth during a mismanaged forceps delivery. During and after this work I would experience extreme coldness, which seemed to be the effect of shock being released. The fact that the bones of my face had been locked together not only explained the sinusitis, but might even throw light on why singing had always been so difficult.

The benefits of this work are many. At one level it can free us from aches, pains and restricted movement. At another it releases energy locked away in emotional and physical trauma. This work also allows us to *re-member* parts of ourselves, see events in a new light and resolve stressful contradictions, becoming more integrated in the process. It is possible that through this cellular memory we may inherit wisdom, not only from our great-grandmothers and their grandmothers before them, but from a long line of women stretching back to ancient times. That is if we are open to it.

There are other ways of opening to this kind of knowing. We can explore it by tracking our intuitions back to their roots. To do this we need to start, once again, by remembering who we are, this time in a physical sense of re-membering – limb by limb, body part by body part, cell by cell. Until we learn to respect and love our bodies we will not receive the messages they are ready to give us.

BEFRIENDING YOUR BODY

Women's bodies are glorious in their shapeliness and diversity, yet the majority of women I know find it hard to like their bodies. What has gone wrong? The media, consumerism and old messages from school or family conspire against women liking themselves as they are. Glossy magazines promote the myth that the small, sanitised and made-up body is beautiful. Fashion consultants tempt ordinary women to have makeovers. How often do you look at the before and after photographs, know what you are supposed to think, but secretly prefer the 'before' picture? Mail order catalogues try to sell us endless gadgets to reduce fat, eliminate body hair and generally whip our bodies into shape. Some women opt to ignore their bodies instead, but giving up disguise and discipline and substituting neglect is just another way of punishing the body.

Instead we need to learn to love our bodies. This came home to me while looking through old photographs. At 50 I was looking back enviously at the body I had disliked at 40. At 40 I had wished for my 30-year-old body. It struck me that I had only ever loved my body in retrospect. Why not appreciate it in the here and now?

This is easier said than done. Quite apart from the fashionable benchmarks of the time, there are so many ways for our constantly changing bodies to be 'unacceptable'. No sooner is a child happy with a lithe, athletic body than it grows breasts that bounce uncomfortably as she runs. Menstruation means that we not only bleed but have mood and energy swings. Being pregnant can be like inhabiting a new body – we may have a heightened sense of well-being or we may experience sickness or heartburn. Then suddenly our breasts, which may have been 'too small', become 'too big' as we breast-feed. Later come the often dramatic changes of the menopause, followed by the ageing process as our skin loses elasticity and wrinkles begin to appear.

Sadly we have been conditioned to look upon almost all of these phenomena negatively. Try re-framing just one of these so-called negative experiences: If you have no energy or disabling cramps during your period, don't feel guilty because you want to crawl into bed with a hot water bottle. Accept it. Do it. Respect it as a message from your body about the importance of turning inward at that time and having slow, reflective, woman time alone with your body.

Our body is never boring and is capable of so many life-giving functions as we move through these cycles. The experience of having a heart scan filled me with awe. It was extraordinary to look into my own body via the screen and to see my own heart pumping away. It was so unremitting in its energy, so consistent – of course! But also a miracle of perpetual motion that this small organ had been driving this great body hour by hour, day in, day out for 55 years. My heart went out to my own heart in gratitude.

EXERCISE – APPRECIATING YOUR BODY

Put some time aside – at least half an hour. Make the usual preparations.

Identify 3 parts of your body, at least one of which you have found it hard to enjoy in the past.

Spend some time tuning in to each part and understanding how it feels fulfilling the function it does.

Now write at least five appreciations of each part and take time to thank the part for doing what it does, and to admire and respect it.

Keep this record to hand and revisit the exercise from time to time, especially if you find it difficult to be whole-hearted in your admiration of any body part.

TUNING IN TO YOUR BODY

Your body is a sensitive instrument capable of virtuoso performance. It has a fine radar system, a vast memory and a remarkable communication network. It needs care if it is to work well. Yet we frequently neglect our bodies, while at the same time being careful to put the correct fuel in our cars and to service them regularly. Our bodies also need the correct fuel, regular detoxification, rest and holidays, as well as all the tender loving care we can give them.

Start by making friends with your body and nourishing the senses.

SIGHT

Feast your eyes on small things like rain on spiders' webs or the shape and colour of vegetables. Take an ant's eye view occasionally or imagine yourself as a visitor from another planet to give yourself 'fresh eyes'. We rely so much on sight that we no longer really 'see' familiar scenes. Goethe, the 18th century German writer, philosopher and poet, used to hang his pictures upside down in order to see them in a new way. That way it is easier to see the relationships *between* things, rather than the subject matter. Similarly you can experiment with standing on your head or bending over and taking a view through your legs. Have a bit of fun trying out these ideas.

SOUND

Give your hearing a treat by listening to music both wild and gentle, and to the natural sounds of water and wind. Exercise your voice and feel it vibrate within your body. Your voice is capable of a huge range of sound and volume. Look for opportunities to let it rip, singing in the shower, in the car, shouting into the wind or simply having a good "*yippee!*" when you are happy.

SMELL

Take delight in the natural smells around you. Why do you dislike the odours you experience as unpleasant? What is so special about your favourite smells? Collect essential oils to enjoy in the bath or in a burner. Take some time when alone to get to know your own body smells. Modern habits of showering frequently and using deodorants mean that many of us rarely experience our own natural aroma. The sense of smell is particularly evocative. When you come across a smell that conjures up a memory, take some time to explore that snapshot or episode in your life.

TASTE

Slowly savour the taste of your favourite food. Gradually cut down on salt and artificial flavourings, so that your palate starts to appreciate natural flavours. Notice how smell and colour affect taste. In a very real sense we are what we eat and drink. Tune into your body to know what it needs. The difference between needs and cravings will soon become apparent. What is nourishing and cleansing? What clogs the system and drains energy? Would you benefit by reducing your intake of caffeine, alcohol or sugar? Or by eating raw vegetables and fruit to gain energy, lose weight and get rid of toxins? I refer you to Leslie Kenton's writings about raw foods to find out how to enjoy such a diet and to understand why it works.[5] Remember that the emotion that accompanies food is just as important as the food. Don't eat when you are upset or rushed. Aim to focus positively on how the food is nourishing you.

TOUCH

Bring the sense of touch into focus by closing your eyes and exploring your desk, your living room. Walk barefoot on dewy grass. Wear silk next to the skin. Include other sensuous fabrics in your wardrobe such as velvet, soft wool, coarsely woven linen or cotton. Think of the touch you exchange with others. Is there enough of it? Or too much? Is it appropriate? Do you enjoy it? Think about what you need and how you might ask for it from people you trust. Consider having a regular massage session, massaging your feet while you watch TV or exchanging a massage with a friend or partner. In the shower, breathe out slowly and relax your pores until you have a sense of the heat of the water fizzing into your veins. Try this as you direct water onto the back of the neck along the hairline as an excellent treatment for a headache.

BREATH, MOVEMENT, SENSUALITY

Breathing is something we take for granted. It's easy to neglect but doing it well increases energy and reduces stress. Breathing deeply is a route to being 'in your body' just as the inability to take a deep breath is a sure sign of being 'out of your body'. To break this tension, concentrate on exhaling first. Breathe out and out and out, expelling the breath by contracting your belly and diaphragm until you are desperate for air. Then relax and suck in air deeply and gratefully. Repeat until you are fully relaxed and able to inhale deeply in a more 'normal' way. Singing, walking and swimming will all help you to breathe more deeply. Disciplines such as Tai Chi and Yoga teach conscious attention to breathing.

Dancing is another way to use breathing in an unconscious way, as well as raising energy, releasing tension and improving circulation. Some people take naturally to moving to music. Others struggle as I did. The instruction to let the movement come from within made sense at a head level, but it was a long time before I 'got it' at a gut level. From my experience I would say that it is worth persisting along the lines of 'fake it to make it!' At first I was conscious of having to work out a movement that went with the music and which I could repeat without feeling too self-conscious. Then one day I was feeling too tired and preoccupied to do that. I stood there worrying about managing a piece of forthcoming work and without thinking found that I was taking it into the dance. I was dancing the problem, my feelings about it and eventually a growing confidence in a way forward. By the end of the dance my tiredness had vanished. I felt exhilarated and full of energy. The work went well the following week.

Belly dancing is a particular form of dance ideally suited to tuning in to body rhythms. It originated in the Middle Eastern palaces of Arabia, Egypt and Turkey where the women of the harem danced for their own pleasure. It was not, as is commonly thought, an entertainment for men. Belly dancing brings together sequences of specific steps and gestures which loosen the joints, stretch muscles and massage inner organs. Simultaneously they loosen inhibitions, stretch our self-imposed limitations and massage our sense of woman-self. Developing the skill requires both discipline and abandon. The learner needs to learn precise movements, to make them uniquely her own and to practise them until they become second nature. In putting them together however, she needs to let go and allow her body and the music to lead. Women wear ankle chains and foot jewellery and tie colourful scarves decorated with tiny gold coins around their hips to emphasise their gyrations. This is where the fuller figure really comes into its own.

With or without belly dancing a harem evening is a wonderful way of bringing women together. Arrange plenty of big cushions, blankets and towels in a carpeted area. Light candles and incense and play suitable music. Women can bring colourful scarves or fabric to drape over pictures, television and furniture to transform the space. Activities can include dressing up, exchanging hand and foot massage, manicures, making each other up, henna body painting, braiding hair or sewing in a circle while telling stories.

For an activity that gives all the senses a treat put time aside for a luxury bath. Light candles, arrange flowers and lay out fluffy towels and soothing lotions. Prepare a favourite drink and light snack, select some relaxing or inspiring music and run the water with aromatic oils. Turn off the telephone and enjoy! Consider this as a ritual to perform in the days before a period to ease premenstrual tension (see next chapter).

Above all, *listen to your body's wisdom*. Listen to its messages about hunger and thirst, rest and exercise, stimulation and relaxation. Where are the areas of discomfort and tension? Are all systems functioning well? Notice when you are tired and take a nap. Even ten minutes will leave you refreshed. Identify times in the day when you can take mini 'time-outs'. A top executive in an international oil company I worked with used to set his watch to beep on the hour. When it beeped he would close his eyes for one whole minute and open them, refreshed. Think about the breaks you do have – are they healthy for you? How could you improve them? If you take a holiday, make sure it really is a holiday – for you and not for someone else – and leave your mobile phone and laptop behind.

EXERCISE - PLEASURE EXERCISE

Put some time aside – about ten minutes is enough. Try to ensure that you will not be disturbed. You will need your notebook and a pen.

Breathe deeply to relax yourself and become present in your body.

1. On a piece of paper rule 5 columns, making the second column much wider than the other four.

2. In the first column number down from 1 to 10.

3. In the second column list 10 activities that give you pleasure.

4. In the third column indicate roughly how much each one would cost. It might be anything from £0 for smelling a rose, through £1 sign for eating chocolate, to several £££ signs for a trip to the opera.

5. In the fourth column show approximately how long it would take to obtain enjoyment from it. Listening to music can take 5 minutes but it might only give true pleasure if you were to immerse yourself in it for an hour.

6. In the fifth column record when you last enjoyed this pleasure.

> 7. How often do you give yourself pleasure? Is it time you made a pleasure date with yourself?
>
> 8. Choose a pleasure to treat yourself to today and at least another two for the weekend.
>
> 9. Make a commitment to work through the list on a daily basis and to add to it as new pleasures occur to you.

All of these approaches are designed to make you feel at home in your body and help you to love and respect it. They all nurture our fertile creativity. Just as preparing the soil, germinating the seed, weeding and providing the right combination of light, heat, shelter and water nurture a crop, so giving attention to our own bodies and minds grows our creative potential.

We may bring the richness of that potential to the work of creating music or painting a picture. We may take it into a valued friendship or an intimate, loving sexual relationship. We may pour our creative energy into paid work or use it in the arts of home-making or housekeeping. We may decide to devote it to the process of raising children. Or we may involve ourselves in any combination of these. Whatever we choose, the energy we use is the same. It is of the body, earthy, sensual and infinitely fertile.

ANCIENT AND MODERN BODY

Your body has answers to all sorts of life questions. Ask it and take time to listen. If you have an area of discomfort or pain, take the time to relax and tune into that part. If your knee hurts, make your way, as it were, inside the joint by travelling through your body. Ask it what it needs to heal. The answer may come in different ways – an image, a sensation or feeling or words. It may be about a life change you need to make or something simpler like a hot bath or a cold pack of frozen peas. Louise Hay [6] and Gill Edwards [7] provide lists of associations for ailments throughout the body that may help you to understand what message your body may be sending. They set the body part or complaint alongside a life meaning and suggest an affirmation to help restore a healthy balance. Although these are useful tools and help the process along, there is no substitute for asking your own body, for everyone will have an individual reason for having a common symptom.

Jan took the opportunity in a small group session at a workshop to explore the paralysis problem which may have started on that day in the garden with her father.

> *"I would freeze in difficult situations at work when I needed to respond quickly to challenge or criticism. I knew I'd uncovered something significant when the work released a wave of emotion. It came breaking through the paralysis. It showed up physically in an overwhelming migraine. Eventually I had to go to bed for the rest of the day, but it felt worth it. I knew I'd made some real progress."*

A migraine is always a compelling piece of communication from the body that should not be ignored. An image or body sensation will often accompany whatever message your body sends. For Jan it was a boggy entity she called 'Squidge' located in her stomach, which she recognised as a barometer for critical emotions she was picking up in a situation. Squidge acted as an early warning system, alerting her to an issue that needed attention.

Giving your image a name helps to make it your friend and is an opportunity to bring some humour to the process. Whenever this same image appears in future, pay attention and dive into the uncomfortable feeling, rather than try to ignore and rise above it. This habit can move us on by helping us to allow body knowledge. In this way we can gradually learn to trust our gut in all situations of decision-making and conflict.

Jan was familiar with migraine headaches as indicators of deeper problems. Crippling migraines accompanied her periods in her late thirties:

> "The period itself was not problematic, but the headaches would last three or four days. It'd move from one side of my head to the other – left, right, left again, reaching a crescendo on the third day. They left me wiped out, and I seemed to be losing one week in four out of my life. I went to my GP and eventually ended up by a roundabout route with a marriage guidance counsellor. Pretty soon she asked me how I got on with my mother. I told her fine. Which was true as long as we didn't talk about anything that mattered. I was quite confident that this wasn't the problem. Then all of a sudden came these hot angry tears, I couldn't stop. I was amazed! But I was even more amazed that the migraines stopped after that and never came back. I've had the odd one since then but never a regular pattern."

Learn to regard minor ailments and illnesses as messages from your body. Instead of being annoyed or depressed at being laid low, ask, "what is my body telling me here?" If you have a sore throat, check whether there is something you are not saying to someone in your life. A stiff neck? Is someone a pain in the neck to you? Is some straight talking required? Is your body simply insisting on a rest? Or does the problem go much deeper than that?

Most of us have addictions, whether they be to caffeine, alcohol, chocolate, nicotine or *Eastenders*. It may be that you are ready to move into a new phase of your life in which habits that have served you well up until now are no longer relevant. In fact, you need to get rid of them. As our bodies age and as we pay more attention to being spiritually conscious, our systems become less tolerant of these addictions. Without them your system will be cleaner and the messages from your body clearer.

MESSAGES IN METAPHOR

The body often communicates in metaphor. Metaphor literally means to 'carry across' and is able to convey the spirit and intention of a message through analogies and images in a way that more factual language could not. For example, my acupuncturist once said to me, *"your fire energy is low and when that happens, because your element is earth, you get all soggy like a marsh from the water. The earth needs the fire to keep it warm and fertile."* Although I had only a hazy idea of the system of elements and energy meridians that acupuncture uses, I understood because the description mirrored how I felt.

Metaphor is a very individual thing – one woman's metaphor will not fit another woman's experience. For example, Nina described herself as "shrinking into her bones" when she felt vulnerable, and moving outward to fully inhabit her skin when she was dancing. Nina's phrase "in my skin" didn't at first make sense to Anita. For her, living at skin level meant skating on the surface, feeling brittle and disconnected. To fully inhabit her body, Anita needed to sink down into her bones. They were both describing similar states but differing life experiences led them to express it in contrasting ways. Exploring the detail of this kind of metaphor can lead to useful insights.

EXERCISE – BODY METAPHORS

Put some time aside – at least half an hour. Make the usual preparations.

Make a list of the body metaphors you tend to use most
(e.g. "it gets up my nose" or "she's a pain in the backside")
and reflect upon how they relate to your commonly occurring symptoms or ailments.

> What messages does this give you?
>
> Are there issues that need resolving or unfinished business that needs dealing with?
>
> Choose the symptom that troubles you most and describe the key issues linking with it.
>
> Map out a strategy for behaving differently.
>
> Commit to putting this strategy into action and make a date or dates in your diary.
>
> Enlist the support you need to do this. Who will listen, challenge or encourage you?
>
> Identify appropriate ways to reward yourself.
>
> Notice how your health improves, or, if it doesn't, explore how you are avoiding the issue or missing the point in subtle ways.

Exploring the body's use of metaphor is a way of accessing deeper and deeper layers of body knowing. We become aware of this knowledge through twinges and discomfort indicating emotional or physical disease. We can take this further by recognising how physical symptoms link to our life purpose, as in the work of Louise Hay [8] and Gill Edwards [9] already mentioned. But the body is also capable of a much deeper knowing from a more ancient source. For instance, our bodies carry memories of past lives. This may seem surprising until we consider that modern cosmology tells us we come from the stars. Donna Ladkin, Visiting Fellow at Bath University, describes our cells as old cells *"retaining a longer memory, one that spans all quantifiable notions of time and space."* [10]

At a women's workshop some years ago I gained a real sense of this timelessness of body memory. As a group we were guided in meditation deep into our bodies and I found myself travelling as if through an endless tunnel of time. I was being greeted and supported by women from increasingly distant generations. We shared strongly felt common bonds and connected to a source of loving renewal.

This kind of activity gives us access to what Donna calls her *"deep earth body"*, which is ancient and tuned in to the rhythms of the universe. For women, the most ancient source of knowing is through our menstrual blood which is regulated by the cycles of the moon, and which was used for centuries in sacred fertility rituals.

I was particularly slow to acknowledge the significance of my menstrual cycle to my creativity. But the body can be very persistent in getting its message through, hammering away at our consciousness until we eventually notice. I was attending a monthly research group whose members were exploring their working process in a holistic way. The women in the group remarked upon the fact that our cycles had started coinciding with the meetings. Still I failed to notice the significance of this in spite of the exuberance of my periods at that time. Then I dreamt that a small fiery dragon curled up in my bleeding stomach. Dragons symbolise the fiery creativity of women which is closely associated with fertility, sexuality and menstruation. The dream brought it home to me that I was meant to be examining the meaning of menstruation in our lives.

What would your Wise Woman do?

She would soak in a deep bath and massage her feet.

Then she would know what to do.

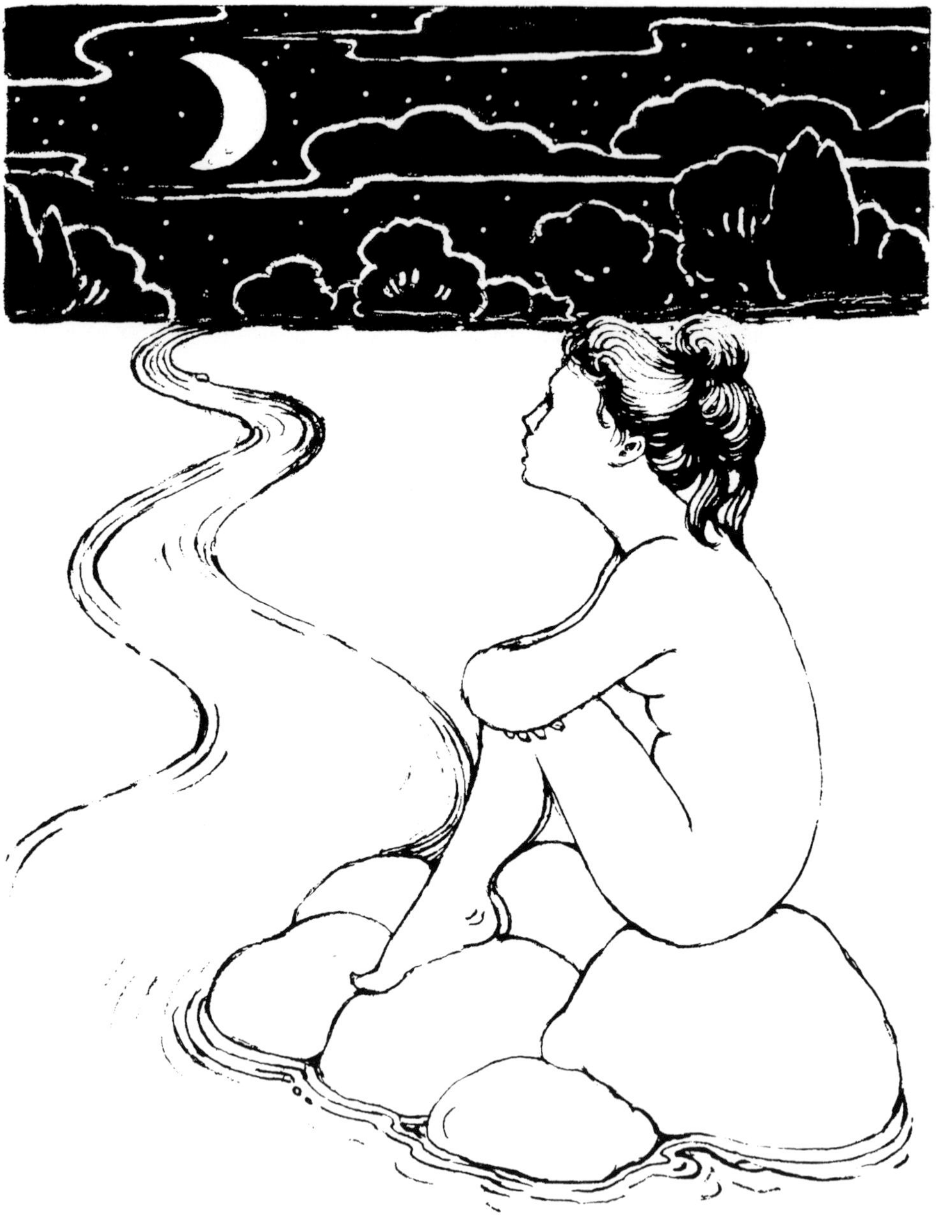

– CHAPTER 8 –

THE MAGIC OF MENSTRUATION

"... imagine that when you bled you were able to use the psychic powers that open and become available to you at this magical time of the month."
Vicki Noble [1]

The richest and most obvious source of body wisdom for women is our menstrual cycle. It sets us apart from men, linking us to other women and to the phases of the moon. The origin of the words for the menstrual cycle, the moon, month and the moon goddess Minerva are ancient and intertwined, while the first calendars that measured time were based on women's menstrual cycle as much as 3000 years ago.[2] Scientific evidence shows that the moon rules the ebb and flow not only of the oceans, but also of our body fluids.

The ebb and flow of light and darkness in the skies is mirrored in the ebb and flow of energy during our cycles and explains the undulation of moods we experience. It is *normal* if we have less active, outward energy between ovulation and bleeding. It is *natural* if we turn inward at this time when we are most attuned to inner knowing and *"have greater access to our magic".*[3] Our dreams may be more vivid during this phase and we may find that tears and anger come more readily. There is a message in this. It is not that we feel more at this time, but that important issues come closer to the surface and we are less prepared to be accommodating and repress them. It is a time for reflecting upon and dealing with situations that need attention in our lives.

If we look more closely at the phases of the moon and how they correspond to the cycle of growth of the seasons, it may be easier to understand the fluctuations in our energy, moods and needs throughout our cycle. The new moon is like a seed at the time of sowing. Then it waxes and grows into flower at full moon, moves into the fruitful time of harvest in the last quarter, and finally into a compost or reflective phase before the cycle starts again. A useful tool for reference in developing this awareness is the We'moon diary which is published every year.[4]

Ironically, I only came to value the richness of the bleeding time, which brought greater creativity and more availability to the influence of the 'other world', when I was already moving into menopause. However, the insight that the menstrual cycle is, potentially, a sacred link to creativity changed my attitudes and prompted me to talk to other women about their experience.

New habits of thinking take some practice. Revaluing menstruation involves moving it away from being unmentionable and embarrassing, towards being discussible. In the process we need to let go of shame and embarrassment in order to become comfortable with such discussion. This chapter and the next explore the experience of a number of women in a way that breaks taboos (in the modern sense of the word), not in order to shock or offend, but in order to honour the taboo in the ancient sense of the word as *sacred*. This exploration uncovers and releases meanings that have become obscured and distorted. For some individual women this may lead to a process of discovering the transpersonal or spiritual through the deep physical connection with ancient roots.

For other readers some of the material may be disturbing. You may prefer not to read on. If that is the case, simply notice why you are making that choice. I faced a dilemma in reporting the following discussion of menstruation. Was the unedited version too strong to publish? What if I edited some passages? Eventually I decided that by editing I would be colluding with the very social convention I was aiming to challenge. I do not want to force images on an unwilling reader. I do want to demonstrate that it is appropriate, natural and a great relief for some women to discuss this sensual subject in a sensual way. The conversation takes place between women who know and trust each other in the intimate environment of a women's group.

They all agreed to share that experience with other women through the medium of this book.

Imagine that we are eavesdropping this group who meet regularly and know each other well. This evening they have agreed to discuss the subject of menstruation. They will be talking about the preparation they were given as children; their first period; their general experience of menstruating; how menstruation is sacred and the menopause. Two members of the group are starting the session by taking it in turn to read extracts from books they have found interesting:

> *"... during that time a woman lives much closer to self-knowing than usual; the membrane between the unconscious and the conscious thins considerably. Feelings, memories, sensations that are normally blocked from consciousness pass over into cognizance without resistance."* [5]

> *"... deep down in every woman's process, there is an unconscious pull to remember the ecstasy of this ancient, sacred encounter with the forces of the earth and sky coming through her body. And ... she had been socialized ... to be afraid to manifest such a longing. Is PMS so surprising?"* [6]

> *"Menstruation is a time which is absolutely taboo in the most ancient sense of the word, which means 'sacred'. ... It is, for humans, the major magical event of the lunar month, corresponding to the waxing and waning cycle of the moon and the ebb and flow of the oceanic tides."* [7]

> *"Imagine a world in which menstrual blood was once again accepted as a magical fluid with the power to nurture new life."* [8]

There followed an outburst of exclamations:

"If only!"

"It isn't like that for me!"

"What about the pain?"

"And the mess!"

"Your period sacred and magical! Isn't that exciting?"

"It's certainly different!"

"It is exciting, but it's scary too. It's kind of hard to take on board."

"THE TALK"

The women go on to talk about the information they were given before they started their periods. Several mothers had consciously tried to improve on their own experience a generation earlier:

> Laura: *"It was quite open for me, I remember my Mum giving me a talk, when I was about 11: 'you might get your periods', and I was delighted! I remember saying, 'how much blood?' and being told a couple of spoons and we had a talk about how much exactly."*

> Verity: *"I think my information came from teenage magazines and the playground with other girls more than my Mum. And I remember that my grandmother gave me a book, and I remember finding that really informative, really helpful. And that's about it really."*

> Lesley: *"What happened to me – I remember sitting having tea together as a family, and my Dad must have been primed, and my dad and my brother disappeared and my mother gave me a fact sheet from a magazine and said something like, 'it's about time you read this'. She left the room while I read it, and she came back and said, 'have you got any questions?' I just said 'no'. And that was it. 'Any questions?' Very brisk. No emotions attached. It was a big step for her considering how it was for her and she wanted it to be different, didn't want me to go through what she had. Mum told me that she wasn't told anything and*

when she started she thought she was dying."

Laura: "My mother had a horrible time. I remember her describing how nobody told her anything. She didn't know what was happening. She described her sister getting it and thinking she was dying. So I think she really had that awareness. I can feel the step from her generation, very different."

FIRST TIME

The women go on to recall their first time, some remembering more vividly than others. Some mothers were closely involved, others kept a distance. Daughters sometimes felt ambivalent about the closeness or actively avoided it. It might be tempting to be treated as an adult, but if there had been no previous sharing, this sudden intimacy in such a personal context was too much:

Laura: "I was staying at my friend's house and I woke up. I remember it was such a dark colour! I had cramps like diahorrea and I thought – what's this, I've gone in the bed! What am I going to do? And my friend's mother, who I knew really well, she realised before I did. I didn't connect what I'd heard with the way it was. And I do know I felt very washed out and weak. I felt very – I knew it was big, in fact it reminds me a bit of when I lost my virginity, the same feeling of like, 'I feel different'. My body felt so different, and I think I was quite happy about it, but it was much more powerful than I had imagined.

"It was amazing because it was the day before my twelfth birthday and my mother also got her first period the day before her twelfth birthday, and that really made me thrilled!"

Lesley: "What I remember was waking up in the morning and I thought I'd messed my pyjamas. And at school the school secretary came and took me up to the sick bay. 'Your Mum has been on the phone. She found your pyjama trousers. In case you need anything, here it is in the cupboard, and you can just come back and get it and come and lie down if you need to.' And she was so lovely, that made me feel special. But I didn't have any sense of what was happening in my body. Some of my friends had already started so I was very glad to go in and whisper 'I've started', but I didn't enjoy it, I wasn't glad."

Alex: "I was very late. I was the last one to get my period. I remember looking in my underwear and there was blood and I knew exactly what it was because we'd had the film. I think I was fifteen. Was that impossibly late? 15? I'd had the film when I was eleven! Mum had given me the talk three years before. Everyone I knew had started. It was, 'phew! Thank god it's come!' I'd been checking my underwear for months, maybe years. I remember really wanting to hide it. I didn't want anyone to know, didn't want my parents to know. I phoned my friend up and told her, but I remember taking my clothes down and sticking them in the washing machine. I dealt with it all myself and then, maybe a couple of months later, my mother noticed that my knickers had blood in and said, 'you've got your period' and I was just horrified. 'Mum don't. God. Don't!' I didn't want her to have anything to do with it. And she said, 'oh, you're a woman now.' And I can see now, looking back, that it really meant something to her, and that was all she could say: 'you're a woman now.' "

Chrissie: " I was very matter of fact about it. Got on with it. I never had any problems, any cramps. It was very kind of scientific. I was the first in my class, first to have breasts, first to have this, and I was so capable, and I was dealing with it like I was running a race or something. I was going to be good at this because I was really good at running. I went to find my Mum and told her and she was running the race with me: 'OK right, let's get on with this', discussing it with me, nice intimacy, but also a disgust. I didn't want her that close to me. It was like it was mine and I didn't want my parents to interfere in it or have anything to do with it. And it was a relief that finally I was like everybody else now, grown up."

Pam: *"I was first to menstruate of all my friends. I was camping and I always had navy blue pants so I missed the brown stage! Suddenly it was bright red all over the toilet, and my memory of it was that I thought I was dying and it was like an explosion. I didn't think of the curse, because the curse was just a word and it didn't mean anything. I was suddenly really important – my mother rushing up to the chemist. And trying to get this belt thing on and not knowing how to fix it and my Mum was there showing me how it worked.*

"I kind of felt important, important with myself. Didn't feel like it was celebrated in any way by anyone. I was eleven and I felt quite important and I was able to tell my friends. And then my sister started, she's two years younger than me, and she had the most awful pains and she was physically sick and that kind of took over from my important periods. It was like Jen's 'Really Important Periods'. My mother went berserk looking after my sister, hot water bottles. My sister has always been more dramatic than me."

Verity: *"My memory of it is really vague. I don't remember when I started. I think I was between eleven and twelve but I don't remember the moment. I do remember a girl at school I was friendly with. We always promised to tell each other as a secret on the telephone when we started. And by the time mine started I'd fallen out with her. And it felt really sad. But I don't remember, don't remember. My Mum died when I was twelve and I can't really remember whether they started before or after she died even. I think they started before she died but I don't really remember telling her. Very, very vague. No celebration!"*

Other women talked of grey or blurry memories or didn't remember at all. These are what Kami McBride[9] would consider *"dangerous answers"*, because they show a disconnection with the body and its cycles which tends to lead to difficulties with self-image and associated physical problems. Verity's experience of sadness in mid-pregnancy echoes this. She describes having treatment from a cranio-sacral osteopath:

> Verity: "... he felt that my sadness was really connected inside to my menstruating. And he did something in my body, said he was lifting a veil of sadness from my body, and he thought it was connected to my cycle."

These accounts leave us in no doubt about the importance of this transition into womanhood for all women. Although the initiation was not marked with any kind of ceremony, the evidence is there in the women's eagerness to talk and in the emotional charge of the memories, whether they are vague or vivid. One of the women went on to start thinking about what they could do to give their daughters a better experience. She read:

" 'How might it have been different for you, if, on your first menstrual day, your mother had given you a bouquet of flowers and taken you for lunch ... and then you went ... to the Women's Lodge, to learn the wisdom of the women?'[10] How's that for a different cultural message? Changing from taboo meaning don't mention it, to taboo meaning special, sacred."

> "That's lovely, I wish I'd known enough to do something like that for my daughter."

> "Me too."

> "That's something to think about. I've still got time to do it for mine!"

Lesley sounded a note of caution, a warning against being over idealistic about the menstrual experience:

> "How authentic is it really to say, 'whoopee! This will happen to you for the next forty years?'"

Certainly it is important not to minimise the inconvenience or possible pain and discomfort. Many women experience menstruation as boring, unpleasant or distressing. On the other hand, women have the opportunity to redress the balance of the overwhelmingly negative messages of the past, and frame the bleeding time more positively for their daughters.

EXERCISE – INITIATION RITUAL

Put some time aside – at least half an hour, preferably more. Make the usual preparations.

What is your memory of your first period? How, if at all, was it marked?

Imagine what you would have liked to happen. Invent a ritual or a treat that would make you feel special in this respect. Choose something that you can do now, a retrospective marker to make up for what didn't happen in the past.

If you have a daughter, think about how you could create a ritual together that she would appreciate.

COPING WITH MESS & PAIN

Next the group share the ambivalence of the experience of menstruating over the years:

> **Lesley:** *"I hated all the apparatus, sanitary belts and towels with loops. It was so uncomfortable, and I had quite heavy periods so that was a drag. I didn't like all that."*

> **Pam:** *"I just remember I was embarrassed because I had a pad in my knickers at certain times of the month and none of my friends did. I did a lot of sport so I always felt that it showed when I was playing hockey or netball."*

Chrissie: *"I remember the acrid smell. The smell. How could this come from my body? Dry and caked and bitter, so strong smelling. It was almost attractive and then disgusting. And I remember at school there weren't any places to put the STs, so you had to go round with this stinky thing in your satchel! And the idea that anyone might find it, open it. Oh god! This smelly thing! What do you do with it? Disgusting! I remember my big satchel and sticking it in there, so that was a really strong memory."*

Lesley: *"I know what you mean, the funny smell. It was disgusting in one way. But in another way it was rather nice, quite comforting somehow. The other thing I remember – they used to loop the STs round the doorknobs in the sickbay to stop the doors banging. We used to get the giggles."*

Most people used the very negatively loaded name of 'the curse' to describe menstruation.

Verity: *"My mother used to only ever refer to it as the curse."*

Pam: *"My Mum, every time she realised I was bleeding, she'd say it was the curse. I never felt it was a curse. I never liked using that word either. My mother was very medical, very practical, and she talked about the curse that was coming, and that's all she ever called it, the curse."*

Kami McBride [11] views these negative names as damaging as they create neural pathways that shape our experience. She believes that this influences our attitudes not only to menstruation but to menopause as well. Finding a positive name (e.g. Moon Time, Red Tide, Sacred Womb Time) is an important part of the work she does with her students. You may like to choose for yourself a name that has more positive impact than labels you have previously used.

Of the more neutral names used by the women in the group, period was the most common. Variations included 'being on', 'on the rag', 'having a friend visiting' and 'my monthly'. A sanitary towel might be referred to as a 'jam sandwich', but no-one recalled any mention of bleeding or blood. That is particularly interesting as the overwhelming impression of these memories is of the shock of the blood. The redness, the dramatic flood of it – alongside the distinctive smell – is what comes back vividly and sensually to so many women.

Yet with the discovery of tampons we no longer have this particular sensual experience each month. See how seductive these tampons are!

> Laura: *"My Mum got me on to the fact that there were tampons quite quickly and I thought, that's exciting! I remember getting very excited about anything new. Diagrams and the rustly paper, so exciting. Like learning how to smoke cigarettes, that kind of feeling."*

> Lesley: *"One thing about tampons, it was a bit like smoking a cigarette because it felt quite illicit. To be talking about them and even considering them with your friends! Eventually trying it and starting to use them! But my Mum didn't provide them and I don't think she used them, so there was that kind of sense of something illicit."*

> Laura: *"Sort of on the way to sex almost."*

> Pam: *"I remember the little case that tampons used to come in, the little plastic one, pink, blue with little starry flowers."*

> Chrissie: *"I always used to find them uncomfortable to use, sometimes painful, really difficult."*

> Alex: *"All my mother ever provided were the belt things. And my sister told me about tampons. Wow! What an idea! Because my sister was doing it, it felt like it was OK. Eventually I told my mother about it, and that was really kind of strange!"*

None of the women in the group had suffered crippling periods such as those experienced by Pam's sister. If that is your experience then you will probably be finding it difficult or impossible to value or even comprehend the mystery involved in menstruating. You may be glad of the mitigating effect of the pill or, like Dorothy, delighted to be free of periods and premenstrual tension during her pregnancy. She certainly did not link her intuition to her cycle:

> "People say to me that I am quite intuitive. In fact my mother-in-law used to call me a witch, because sometimes I know what's going to happen or I know what somebody is going to say next. I don't know why. But as to the menstrual cycle, that's just a pain! I'm just so glad to have nine months off!"

Samantha, an active, energetic woman is even more emphatically negative about menstruation:

As a young woman Samantha had no problem. Her periods were always very light, lasting only a few days. She noticed that friends and work colleagues suffered a range of cramps from minor discomfort to *"most horrendous pains"*, and that pre-menstrual tension (PMT) often left them unable to function.

However when Samantha hit her forties, for her too, menstruation became something to dread each month:

> "As the years passed so did my trouble free monthly cycle. It started gradually with just minor cramps, sore breasts and slight PMT. Then, as if wrinkles, greying hair and strange aches and pains weren't enough to contend with, each month terrible cramps and the most awful PMT lasting 10 days or more, also arrived."

Samantha found the PMT most difficult to cope with:

> "The feeling of complete and utter desperation, misery, and even suicidal thoughts. These also affect my partner who has to live with this monster."

This kind of negative experience is reality for many women and counteracts any attempt to romanticise menstruation. Even those who explore every avenue of treatment, from conventional medication, through complementary therapies to counselling, may not find relief. It reminds us that demons, darkness and depression are part of the human condition, and an essential part of creativity, however unlikely that might seem when we are in their grip.

Having explored both the possibility of menstrual magic and the experience of menstrual misery, it is important to notice that there is also a middle ground. Many women describe their cycle as *'nothing special, but not that bad either'*. It is somehow reassuring to think of these numbers of women going about their daily lives, quietly menstruating and getting on with the business of being a woman without a fuss. Just because there is no drama involved it does not mean that they are any less in touch with their bodies. It simply means that there are countless different ways of experiencing this natural function, all of which are equally valid.

FREEDOM AND CONFLICT

So much of these women's experience focuses on the equipment and logistics of managing a period, rather than on the function of bleeding itself. Using tampons also allows a woman to become distanced from her blood and its odour to some extent. This means less washing and less anxiety, but also less earthiness. The tampon gives us freedom. It is part of the *"technology of suppression"* that allows menstruating women to conceal their periods.[12] This may be vital to success if they are competing in a world dominated by masculine values but, as Lara Owen[13] documents, it may be damaging to their health and their identity as women in the long run.

This conflict between earthiness and mystery on the one hand, and freedom and efficiency on the other, is central to the dilemma of how a woman survives in this culture without becoming less of a woman. If we want to make a special case for women who are menstruating, we run the risk of undermining all the progress towards equality and independence made so far. The alternative is to throw away the importance of the sacredness of that monthly time in favour of behaving 'as normal'. Then the value, integrity and power which is special to women is dismissed, cancelled out and flushed away with the invisible tampon which enables us to swim, wear white trousers or fly aeroplanes as if nothing untoward were happening.

Jan recalls a car journey that highlights the conflict. Normally a highly competent driver, she was aware that on this occasion she lacked fluency and co-ordination:

> *"I completely failed to anticipate other drivers and I kept just missing being in synch with the traffic flow. It all came to a head when I turned out into the path of another car at a roundabout. To make matters worse, I noticed it, regretted it, and so of course I hesitated. I went hot all over with embarrassment, which made me even more flustered. In the end I just accelerated off in confusion. I could just imagine the other driver saying, 'woman driver!' And of course I was only too aware that the comment was hitting its mark! He would have been right for once because I was menstruating!"*

Jan's body needs were in conflict with her planned journey. Her menstrual state was pulling her attention inward in a context where it was essential that her attention be directed outward. Driving is essentially a visual and extrovert activity. It demands an 'up and out' body posture, and outward extension of consciousness to include not only the four corners of the car, but also the position and pattern of movement of other traffic, shape of bends, camber of the road and a multitude of other constantly changing variables. Menstruation on the other hand, is a deeply kinaesthetic experience which demands a pulling in of consciousness and attention to the stomach and genital area, an inturned, even foetal, body inclination, and a tuning in to the twinges and rumblings, smells and internal juices of the body.

Considered in that way it is a miracle that women achieve safe journeys at this time of the month.

Can we really afford to admit that, after all, the time of the month does make a difference? Making such disclosures is risky. Instead we protect others (usually men) from hearing ("I didn't need to know that") or we protect ourselves from being written off as irrational, unreliable, and moody ("it must be that time of the month").

What if we were to schedule our lives *around* our periods instead of the other way round? What if we were to avoid activities involving logic and high performance at that time and allow ourselves some time out for reflection?

What of the practicalities of earning a living? What of the demands of the outside, pacey, male-defined world upon which we depend for that living? How would a corporate career woman cope? Would she see the benefit of such openness or solitary time out? Might she be angry at the implication of vulnerability and the interruption to her high flying life? What if a self-employed woman comes on early in the week when the VAT return must be completed? What if I can no longer predict the date of my period? A lot of anger wells up in me at the cultural twist which has shifted the bleeding time from a pivotal to a peripheral position in the scheme of things that matter.

How would it be to choose a different, inner kind of freedom from that which the tampon symbolises? Luisa Francia describes the freedom of the Tuareg mountain women in Algeria who go without tampons, pads or knickers when they menstruate, partly controlling the flow, partly spreading their legs to let it fall.[14] Of course this may not be practical for reasons of climate and living style as much as social taboo. But this glimpse into another culture offers us another way with a lightness and humour that we probably need if we aim to be primitive and mysterious as well as modern and successful. Our task is to find our own individual and cultural equivalent to the freedom of the

Tuareg women, which will let us value our cycles and benefit from them. We can then live in greater flow and harmony using in appropriate ways the different kinds of energy available to us at each stage of the cycle.

If we pretend that we are not affected by our menstrual cycle we are likely to miss out on the privileges that our bleeding brings, and to neglect the activities that are better suited to that time.

Mamonyia, a young woman in her twenties, has found her own way of compromising simply and without experiencing any particular conflict. Her comment on tampons – that they are both wonderful and awful – reflects an attitude that acknowledges the inwardness of the bleeding time, alongside a need sometimes to be active at that time:

> *"Tampons are awful because my back aches when I use them, but they are wonderful because I can pretty much ignore my period when I need to. If I can be at home I prefer not to use a tampon and to be aware of my flow and of the smell."*

EXERCISE - RESPECTING THE WISE BLOOD

Put some time aside – at least half an hour. Make the usual preparations.

Take some time to consider how you could manage the time of your period differently.

Think about how you could arrange to have a day off or at least a few hours to yourself. Ignore the inner voice that says this is impossible and ask instead: "How might this happen?"
Whose support do you need? Whose demands do you need to refuse? Or is it more a question of giving yourself permission?

> If time off turns out to be truly impossible, reflect upon how you might approach tasks differently at this time. Could you be more intuitive? Might you delegate more? Are you able to schedule quieter, more solitary activities rather than being actively involved with others, in the public eye or doing hard physical work?
>
> How about going to bed early? Drinking less alcohol or caffeine? Finding time to write a journal, record dreams or reflect on the important issues in your life?
>
> Write yourself a commitment to make some meaningful changes and put a reminder in your diary when you expect your next period.

What would your Wise Woman do?

She would know the phase of the moon and tune in to her belly.

Then she would know what to do.

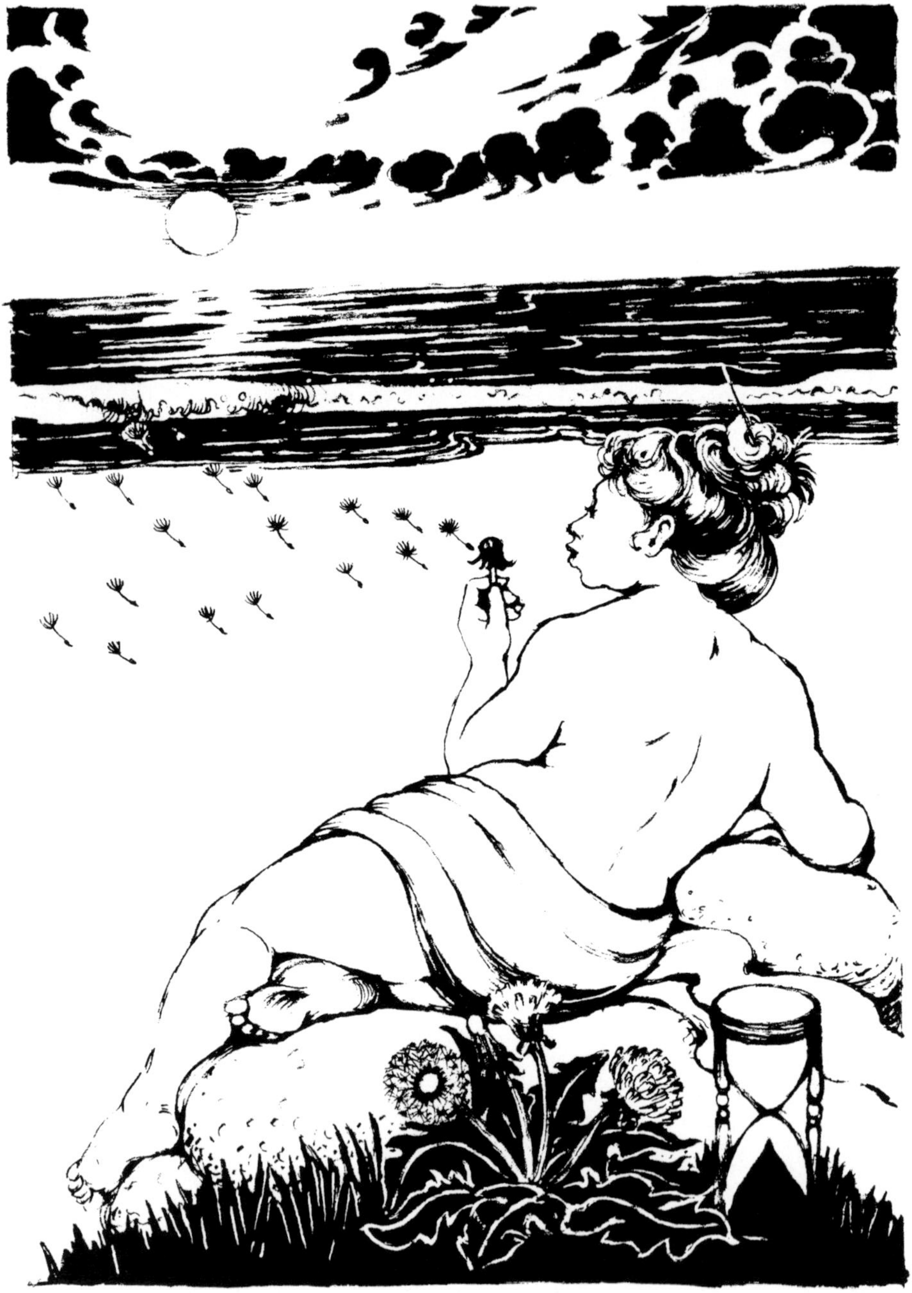

CHAPTER 9

WISDOM, SPIRITUALITY AND MENOPAUSE

"In the Native American tradition a woman is considered to be at her most powerful, psychically and spiritually, when she is menstruating ... on the spiritual planes, gathering wisdom."
Lara Owen[1]

This interpretation of the spiritual significance of menstruation is supported by scientific evidence that *"biological cycles as well as dreams and emotional rhythms are keyed into the moons and tides as well as the planets."*[2] The moon influences our cycle of ovulation by interacting with the electromagnetic fields of our bodies. Exposure to the light of the full moon can trigger ovulation. This meant that when women lived together in the natural settings of traditional cultures, they would ovulate together around the time of full moon and bleed during the period of the dark moon. Even when exposed to electric light, we notice a tendency for modern women to synchronise their cycles when they spend time together regularly. Studies indicate that women are more in tune with their inner knowing at the time of the dark moon and have greater access to their magic, which is their ability to improve things that are not working well in their lives.

It is therefore no coincidence that the time when my periods were demanding attention was also the time when I was searching for a spiritual dimension to my life. It was only much later that I made this connection – when I began to understand the centrality of menstruation to women's wisdom and spirituality.

Women express this special connection in different ways. Mamonyia feels different when she bleeds and recognises her need for time to herself:

"Yes, there's a change in state of mind, though I don't know how to describe it. I think I'm more sensitive. I suppose it's about being more tuned in to my body and so holding the space around me. Protecting that space more. And there's a lot of wisdom in that. It's a time when I would only rarely have sex, prefer not to. And sometimes I like to wake up on my own and have that time to myself. It would be a good time to do that – to arrange to have that space."

Anita describes her deep sense of connection with the moon, which developed when she was twelve years old:

"I was obsessed by the moon, and wrote endless descriptions of moonlit skyscapes, particularly when the moon was full. Now I reflect that this was just before my periods started."

Pam used to welcome her period as a sign of not being pregnant:

"I've always enjoyed them coming. Mainly because from when I was about sixteen I was sexually active and I was worried I was going to be pregnant so I've always really loved getting a period."

However as an adult who is currently not sexually active she continues to appreciate coming on:

"I still get a real buzz out of starting to bleed. Just love it. Mmm."

Mamonyia shares Pam's sense of relief, but again there's more to it than that:

"I love it when my period comes, that first sign of blood feels like a celebration, because I know I'm not pregnant, it's always a relief. Also it seems like a cleansing time, as if the things that have been a problem are washed away. I know that actually they are not necessarily, physically, but there seems to be a clearance, a chance to start again."

The body and psyche are one and as the body releases toxins through the blood, the psyche releases suppressed emotions, a very clear explanation of why women are more sensitive at that time of the month, and how women's spirituality is grounded in the body.[3] However cleansing this process may be, it is not necessarily a positive or welcome experience.

For example, Samantha's experience is both intensely physical, involving disabling stomach cramps; and intensely spiritual, involving a bleak hopelessness in the dark night, or dark moon, of the soul:

> *"Catch me either mid-cycle or just as my period starts and ask me how I feel about the spiritual/cleansing/re-generating aspects of menstruation, and I am afraid that my response would be unprintable."*

This is no airy-fairy spirituality. It taps into the dark, destructive aspects of the feminine that we see in the goddess Kali, the terrible mother who eats her own children.

Menstruation is the place where the sexual, the creative, and the sacred meet, a well-documented link. Ritual blood was thought to possess magical power and in early cultures was used in rituals. In fact the word ritual comes from the Sanskrit '*rtu*' meaning menses.[4]

It was only after men took over from women as priests that sacrifice of animals or enemies became necessary to provide ritual blood, because men lacked their own menstrual blood.[5] The first blood at the altar was menstrual blood, provided by women bleeding together and without the need for sacrifice.[6]

No wonder women often have an ambivalent attitude to the disruption, inconvenience, exhaustion and sometimes even physical shock that periods cause. At one level we cannot cope, we are indignant and protesting: the handicap of being a woman seems outrageous. At another level we can privately revel in the mess and the smells and celebrate the privilege of being a woman. This is not surprising when you consider that our bodies carry the cellular memory of our menstrual blood being used in sacred rituals. This could explain why we feel like showing it off. But of course we don't. 21st century woman cleans up and flushes away until all is immaculate.

Anita reflects on the special feelings that sometimes accompanied her bleeding time:

> *"Sometimes a heavy period used to feel kind of cathartic. I'd feel a sense of emptiness. It was sometimes more like exhaustion, but sometimes peaceful. A bit like I felt after giving birth, only not so intense. But you need to be able to rest and withdraw to get that sense of well-being. Like you just give in and accept that the body function takes over, whether it's feeding a baby or bleeding. You abdicate all other responsibilities, so there are no conflicts, no tensions. Sink into body."*

This descent of a woman into herself has been likened to the descent of the shaman into altered states of consciousness, so that the time of menstruation appears to be a natural time for such explorations. *"Menstruation ... is the precise way in which the human animal is linked to the ... upper world and the underworld of shamanic reality".*[7] One way of tuning in to the 'other world' is paying attention to dreams. In the last years of menstruating I experienced a number of what I call Important Dreams. Plotting these dreams against the moon phases showed an interesting pattern. Although they did not coincide with my periods as I had hoped, they did mostly fall around the time of the dark moon. This is consistent with studies that have shown that the moon influences our dream life. If I had synchronised my cycle with the moon by bathing in the light of the full moon, then maybe I would also have been bleeding.

The characteristics of Important Dreams are that they seem particularly vivid and seem to convey a message. They are more coherent, purposeful and memorable than other dreams, so that the dreamer wakes feeling blessed with a gift or vision. The dream doesn't fade but keeps its colour for days or even years. These dreams are sensuous, using vibrant colours with a luminous quality, movement, metaphor and resonant sound to get the message across. In one dream that stays with me an oriental dancer appeared, whose body was intricately and beautifully painted with snakes in rich colours and gold that gleamed with every movement. This was one of a series of dreams that used the recurring symbol of the spiral. I dreamt repeatedly of spiral staircases, of women with coils of black hair, and of illuminated spirals spinning in and out of a tree like little conical spaceships. Later I came to understand the spiral as a representation of feminine energy and a symbol of the Wise Woman tradition.

Many women find that prophetic dreams emerge at the time of bleeding, erupting into a consciousness that welcomes, notices or invites them. These dreams foreshadow momentous events, although most of us will only be aware of this in retrospect. Some of these dreams seem like a gentle preparation; others give very specific detail as if to draw attention to the importance of the event when it materialises in our lives. For instance, I dreamt of an unusual and elaborately constructed meal. Some months later this meal arrived on my plate. At first the familiarity puzzled me, but when I eventually remembered the dream I recognised the significance of the occasion – a meeting with the man who is now my husband.

Clarissa Pinkola Estés reinforces this need for purposeful solitude to *"invite a conversation between ourselves and the wild soul"*. She attributes a woman's *"premenstrual crankiness"* not just to physical causes, but to the lack of *"time away to revivify and renew herself"*.[8]

We don't normally allow ourselves to 'sink into body' and renew ourselves. Instead we drag our attention out of the body and get into busy mode. We wear uncomfortable clothes and worry about leaking in public. And if we do leak, we see that as our bodies letting us down.

Once in a while, try doing it differently at the time you need it most, whether that is during the premenstruum or in the first days of your period. Try having a ritual bath as described in Chapter 7. Or curl up by the fire with your journal or a book. Or go for a long walk to be alone with your thoughts. Do whatever your body tells you is right for you at this time.

How easy is it to cope with this alternative way of being? Even for women who are incapacitated by their periods, it is somehow easier to lose almost one week in four to pain and incapacity because that is familiar. It feels like self-indulgence to devote even half that time to rest and reflection without interruption from the outside world. It is self-indulgence: indulgence in being fully ourselves, being women. The first step is to break the pattern. It may feel scary or boring or lonely from the outside, but when we actually do it, it feels like coming home. Lara Owen's scientist coped at first by using her 'time-out' as an excuse:

> *"Any excuse to read rather than do chores ... but it didn't take long ... to realize that as soon as I made room at that time amazing things were happening. I would just write prolifically and ideas would flood into my head, strong insights into things, ... a very positive experience."* [9]

EXERCISE - DREAM ACTIVITY

Put some time aside – at least an hour (maybe months!). Make the usual preparations.

Either a) If you are someone who already records your dreams, review your dreams of the last few months.

Select those that you consider "Important Dreams".

Try plotting these against your periods and against the phases of the moon and see if any pattern emerges.

> **Or** b) If you do not have such a record, be patient and spend some months recording your dreams and noting the dates of your periods.
>
> Then plot your dreams as above.
>
> If you have difficulty remembering your dreams, start by giving them more attention. They will usually respond. Keep a pad and pencil by your bed where you can scribble notes or sketches immediately on waking. If you share your bed with another person, explain that you need space when you wake to capture your dreams and bring them across the threshold between sleeping and waking. With time the process will become easier and immensely rewarding. When you look back over your dreams you may see themes or patterns emerging.

EMBRACING MENOPAUSE

A menopausal woman has been described as a wise woman or *"She-Who-Holds-the-Wise-Blood-Inside"*, having gathered wisdom throughout her menstruating life.[10]

And yet we are brought up to think of the menopause as a time when women become a little odd, or at the very least bad-tempered. Not that it is ever discussed. We pick up these messages indirectly from family myths and oblique references to 'that time of life' and 'a woman of a certain age' accompanied by knowing looks. Small wonder that many women approach it with dread as the beginning of the end. Another aspect of loss at this time is the sense that many women have, including myself, of losing something we never properly experienced. In addition, older people are not valued in our culture, and so we face a loss of status and a potential erosion of self-esteem.

As we approach menopause, we can look forward to never having to bother again with tampons and pads, stained knickers and ruined clothes. But then ambivalence creeps in once again. For we also want to hang on to the function that makes us special. Won't we miss this old friend? Won't we be sad to lose the force of this chaos that won't be tamed and modernised into convenience?

Anita reflected that it was only because tampons were useless to contain the flood of her heavy pre-menopausal periods that she once again came into direct contact with the sight and smell of her blood:

> "It was good to be brought up short in a way. To realise that my body wasn't going to be sidelined. And to connect with the earthiness of it all. It was grounding, that's what it was, grounding. It made me realise how out of touch I was with my body. Ignorant too about the hormones and how they worked. I was confused and unprepared for the upheaval."

Like many women Anita didn't understand how her hormones affected her – "What hormones, how do they work?" This question is fully answered by Leslie Kenton[11] in her book about the menopause in a chapter called Cycles of the Moon. She emphasises both the importance and complexity of the interaction of our hormones. *"So central are hormonal events to how women think and feel that it would be no exaggeration to say that the female endocrine system is an interface between body and spirit."* Anita's woman GP was sympathetic but only offered Hormone Replacement Therapy (HRT). Christiane Northrup[12] writes of the distortion of this period of women's life by male gynaecologists who see the menopause as a disease that needs treatment, rather than part of normal female development. She does not underestimate the usefulness of HRT (also discussed by Leslie Kenton in her chapter Crazed Woman), which she herself sometimes prescribes, but points to a number of other ways of alleviating symptoms.

For example, Susun Weed's [13] book on the menopause is an invaluable source of natural strategies and remedies. Weed shows how we are helped in the 'Change' by the fact that it doesn't all happen overnight, but is a gradual process if it happens naturally. The shift breaks down into three phases, before, during and after the cessation of bleeding. Each phase can be seen as a significant stage of transformation into becoming a wise, older woman. Weed sees these phases following the classic stages of initiation: isolation, death and rebirth.[14]

During the pre-menopausal phase (normally between 35 and 55) Weed talks of the need to "fall in love with" regular physical exercise, to gain a little weight (fat cells produce a kind of estrogen and thin women have more hot flushes), and to plan ahead for an extended time alone.[15]

The middle period, or climax phase, brings the transformative lesson of letting go of the Mother identity and doing less caring for others. This is difficult for many women for both practical and psychological reasons. We may uncover hidden frustrations when we put aside this role, as well as experiencing grief, loss and fearful uncertainty about what will replace it. All this will contribute to the *"emotional uproar"* that can accompany night sweats, hot flushes and other physical discomforts.[16] This stage can also be a visionary time and the prime need is for solitude, using a journal to record dreams, emotions and memories, learning to ride the hot flushes and giving attention to diet.

In the post-menopausal years Weed emphasises how natural remedies – herbs, diet and exercise - can alleviate and even reverse troublesome symptoms. If you have completed the second stage by making friends with your own death, the way is clear for the third stage of rebirth. You are ready to be reborn as a wise or whole woman retaining the wisdom of your blood. Be gentle with yourself and bring your creativity to re-inventing or healing your life. At this time I realised that my cycle was still with me. Bleeding had long ceased, but the ebb and flow of energy had settled into a rhythm. I recognised the pattern with gratitude, more alive to the potential of this connection to the moon than I had been before.

Throughout all the stages Weed advocates a gentle, seven step approach to healing, starting with rest and the gathering of information, proceeding to the use of herbs or other natural remedies and only turning to drugs or surgery as a last resort.

THE CRACK BETWEEN THE WORLDS

This is a time when women often become more conscious of that other dimension of life running parallel to ordinary reality. They are more sensitive to the cracks between the worlds and more likely to slip between them into altered states of consciousness, either at will or unexpectedly. This heightened awareness can manifest itself in dreams, meditation, sudden shifts of perspective and noticing synchronicities. The process may happen spontaneously, but we can also encourage it, for example by regular meditation or by giving attention to our dreams.

Anita experienced the other world through experiments with gazing, which led her into an altered state of consciousness. At first this happened unintentionally:

> "I caught my own eye in the mirror while cleaning my teeth and gazed for a long while, retreating and advancing. I found my face dissolving and saw myself as beautiful and unreal. Then came a sense of falling, moving far beyond myself, becoming fearful, but going beyond the fear."

When she tried this on another occasion she noticed a difference between her eyes:

> "The left eye was full of laughter, but the right eye was serious. As I looked into it my face started to dissolve and change with light flickering at the edges. My hair became tawny and my face wrinkled and weather-beaten. Then it seemed furry and lion-like around the nose. Noticing my own fear pulled me back into the everyday but I retained a sense of meeting a wise woman."

Anita then had a dream that echoed these experiences. In the dream she is sitting opposite a woman, a stranger, at a table in a restaurant:

> "I look up to find her gazing into my eyes in a strange and intense way. When I question her silently she says she is looking at my ring — gazing into the stone. And we both know that isn't true, but that it comes to the same thing – going through into another world."

Synchronicities seem to be more numerous at this time because we are open to noticing them. They draw our attention to a pattern and purpose in our lives, which is not usually apparent. We begin to notice coincidence after coincidence leading us in the same direction. All of a sudden the universe seems full of messages delivered by some sort of cosmic highlighting pen. For instance, one morning I woke to see a vibrant green question mark hovering before my eyes. It was a time when I was wrestling with decisions, and this 'vision' felt portentous. Then, as I became more awake and my eyes focused, I recognized the question mark as a long curling tendril of wisteria, which had been growing in the open window for some time and was reaching towards my bed.

Using divinatory cards is one way of stimulating inner knowing and awareness of the parallel dimension. Most people are impressed and fascinated that the cards never fail to be relevant to the question asked or to the person asking, and nearly always give useful insights. This is not so much a way of foretelling the future but of opening up communication with the 'other world'. There is a wide variety of cards available now – tarot, animal, angel, goddess etc. – representing a range of traditions. Choose cards that appeal to you and preferably those that derive from a familiar culture. If you have known the trees and animals depicted from childhood you will have a 'gut response' to them which will otherwise be missing.

REFRAMING SYMPTOMS

As Anita continued into her menopause she was experiencing a time of intense psychic activity. For this reason her view of the world had opened and shifted away from the socially programmed norm. Her perception of the changes in her body was therefore free of the distortion that conditioning brings:

> *"I noticed a phenomenon at night. An experience of a glowing heat pulsating gently and steadily from the very root centre of me. It radiated out and out and out like concentric circles of fire starting in my centre, moving out beyond it to my aura, and breaking through the skin in a sweat. It felt like strong positive energy and my first thought was that maybe this was healing energy beginning to manifest. It intrigued me, not at all unpleasant. Unexpected rather than unwanted."*

Just as she was absorbing this new and exciting sensation, she experienced it in a different situation, when eating out with acquaintances. Immediately she felt uncomfortable, disoriented, claustrophobic, and began to redefine the experience to come into line with how they would define it:

> *"It was **only then** that it occurred to me that what I had framed so positively might be the notorious hot flushes. I was about to feel foolish and relieved that I hadn't mentioned it to anyone when a further thought struck me: 'What if I had never heard of hot flushes?' and 'Did women in early civilisations have hot flushes?'"*

Research suggests that menopausal symptoms may not always be biological in origin.[17] They may have cultural and psychological causes, which does not lessen the discomfort and suffering, but may throw light on how to manage them differently. If, like Anita, a woman can give them a more positive meaning *"her innate healing powers will often be called forth and her symptoms alleviated"*.[18] Christiane Northrup[19] relates how one woman's hot flush was always followed by a flash of insight, and Scilla Elworthy[20] records how hers were always accompanied by a strong emotion and acted like a flag for her attention. Vicki Noble[21] points out that the high body temperature generated can kill off cancer cells and bacteria. By suppressing hot flushes we may interfere with a process we don't understand and damage both our creativity and our health. Leslie Kenton[22] interviewed Dr Leichti von Brausch of the Bircher Benner clinic in Zurich about her experience of menopause. She recalled waking in the small hours in a state of deep sadness and uncovered new ideas when she got up to write about her feelings. Conversations with other women at the clinic revealed similar experiences: *"hidden beneath these feelings lay wells of untapped creativity and bridges to the soul."* Leslie herself discovered that she did her best work at such times.

Anita's insights and experience illustrate the points made by these writers and give us an alternative way of thinking. Prevailing attitudes to older people in general, and to menopausal women in particular, seem to deny women's wisdom just as it comes into its prime. Looked at as the natural development of healing powers, it all feels natural, reasonable and part of a normal progression, no more remarkable or presumptuous than having grey hair or wrinkles and stopping bleeding. This is the stage of the wise woman who uses her experience and the wisdom of maturity to benefit all. She no longer has to focus on her immediate family as a mother must, but has the opportunity to nurture and heal the community and the planet.

EXERCISE - TIME TRAVEL TO WISDOM

Put aside at least half an hour, an hour is better. Make the usual preparations.

Stage 1

a) You are about to go for a spin in a time capsule. Picture it coming to pick you up. Imagine its shape and colour and the sound it makes as it comes in to land. It opens up and you are welcomed aboard. The time capsule takes you five years into the future and sets you down in a new life.

Move around and explore where and how you are living. What can you see around you? Are you outside or in a building? Are you in the country, a town or a village? Are you near water, among trees or in the mountains? Are you in the same country or abroad? Are you alone or with others? How do you spend your time?

When you have fully experienced your new life, take your leave, summon the time capsule and travel back to the here and now. Thank your pilot and return to your body and to the room.

b) Write down and/or draw everything you can remember about life five years from now.

Stage 2

a) Decide what you would most like to materialise from the life you have just visited. Make it into an affirmation – that is, an 'I' statement using the present continuous tense e.g. "I am living in a house by the sea", "I am spending my time writing", or "I am working as a car mechanic". Repeat the statement out loud, say it to yourself as you go to sleep and as you wake up in the morning. Copy it into your journal and write it out every time you use the book.

b) Write down what steps you need to take to make this happen – including the process of negotiation with your nearest and dearest.

Stage 3

Decide whether you are happy to live with this as a pleasant dream or whether you are committed to making it happen. There are no right answers. Be gentle with yourself and remember that you can also change your mind.

What would your Wise Woman do?

She would feel the laughter lines on her face and smile.

Then she'd stop worrying about what to do.

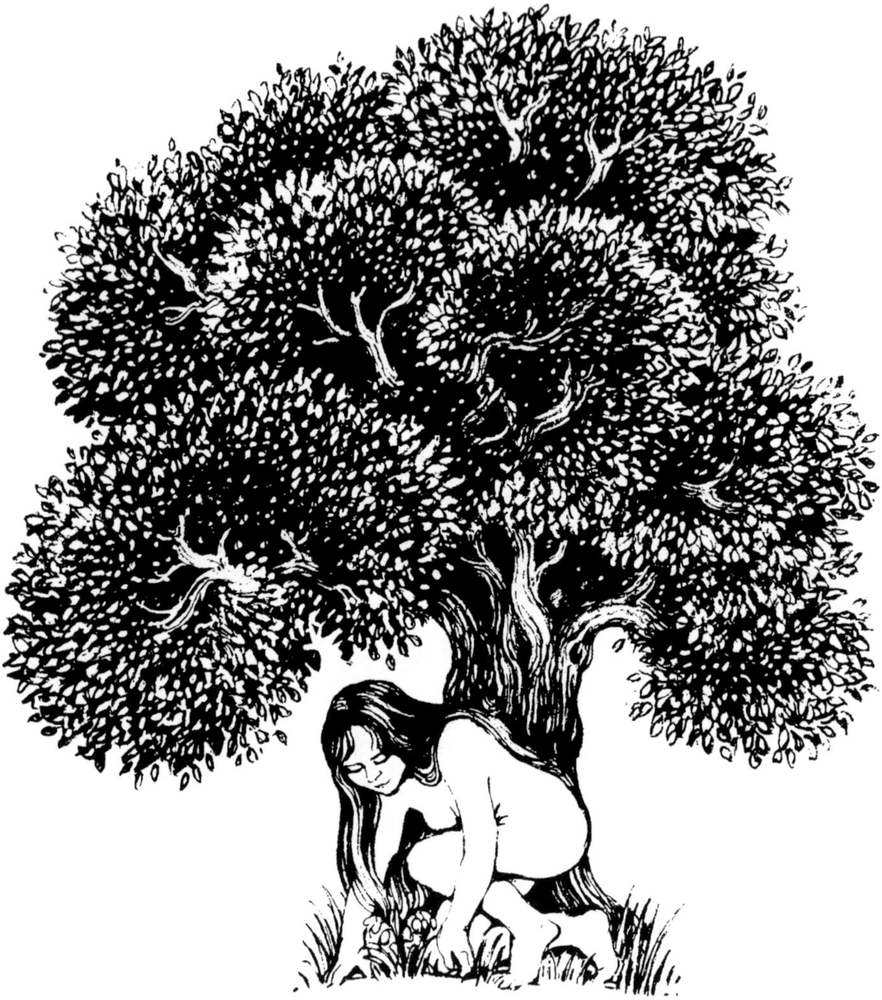

– CHAPTER 10 –

OUR PLACE IN THE NATURAL WORLD

"As human beings we are inextricably meshed in nature. It is the matrix out of which we were born … to which we return at death. … Yet almost everything in modern life would have us forget this fact. The more successfully we forget it, the more alienated we feel from ourselves."
Leslie Kenton[1]

One of the things I like most about our village is that there are no street lights. Visitors from the city often comment on the wonder of looking up to see masses of stars in a dark sky, which prompts me to worry that many people never experience darkness. Some children may never have known a night sky lit only by the moon and the stars. Like half of all Europeans and two thirds of all Americans, they won't have seen the Milky Way with the naked eye because it's obscured by the orange glow of city lighting.[2]

Silence is also hard to come by. Most of us are aware of the background hum of traffic, trains or aircraft alongside various electronic signals or the two-tone blare of sirens. It is a rare luxury to stand on a hillside and soak up a silence accentuated rather than broken by the cry of a buzzard or the hoot of an owl.

It is easy to get out of touch with the seasons and the elements, to lose touch with a natural pace, with seasonal changes and with the daily cycle of light and darkness. Johanna Paungger[3] laments that farmers have lost touch with traditional knowledge of working with the natural rhythms of the moon to increase fertility. Instead they have used harmful fertilisers and pesticides, a strategy that has backfired, resulting eventually in falling yields and impoverished soil. She sees a similar story in medicine and her book is a fascinating presentation of a body of knowledge with which she grew up, and which helps us to work in harmony with natural cycles in all areas of life and to reap the benefit.

Even women, who have such a close connection to the moon, forget to notice its passage from full to dark, as explored in previous chapters. Electricity, central heating, frozen food and airfreight all mean that we can wear the same clothes and eat the same food all year round. The internet and jet travel have shrunk the world so that we lose sight of the vastness of its oceans and land masses. Instantaneous communication, routine trips to the other side of the globe and cheap holidays mean that the world seems less awesome than it did even fifty years ago. All of these things give us the illusion that we are in control. And so we are devastated when natural disasters are able to destroy our civilisations. We are not only physically and emotionally devastated, but spiritually destroyed as well. We are outraged and indignant because we no longer understand our relationship with the natural world, our small part in the system of the whole. We are no wiser than a child who builds a sandcastle on the beach and has a tantrum when the incoming tide washes it away.

For many, civilisation has come to mean 'all mod. cons.', access to motorways, airports and rail links, instant electronic communication, '24/7' shopping and convenience foods. But as the pace has accelerated, as we work longer hours and eat less healthily, stress levels have increased to produce a lifestyle that is far from civilised. Consider, for example, how we travel. Imagine the adjustments that our bodies have had to make in the last two hundred years. From travelling on foot or on horseback our pace has progressively quickened. Cars once travelled at walking pace but can now accelerate to high speed in a matter of seconds. Trains and planes are designed to cut journey times that would have been unimaginable to our great-grandmothers. We expect our bodies to continue to function normally while being hurtled at high speed through time zones in a metal tube.

RECONNECTING WITH OUR ROOTS

Some people apparently thrive at this pace, although we may well ask at what cost and for how long. Others merely survive, and an increasing number suffer dysfunctional stress. There are still others who choose to opt out by moving out of town and changing their style and standard of living. They may be branded as 'going native', 'self-sufficient', 'downsizing' or 'going back to nature'. Although many more people may find it hard to do without the convenience of modern living, they too feel the need to reconnect regularly with natural roots. How can we begin to achieve this?

EXERCISE - NOTICING THE NATURAL WORLD

Put some time aside —say half an hour. Make the usual preparations.

Think of the times in your day when the natural world impinges on your senses.

How often does this happen? Is it most of the time, at frequent intervals or hardly at all? Is it a pleasant or unpleasant experience?

If you work in an environment that is shut off from the natural world, think of how you could bring it into your workplace.

Start to make a point of noticing the natural world in small ways. Is the air cold or damp? What can you smell on the wind or after rain? How many birds can you hear? What's going on in the sky? Try to avoid judging or comparing. Just observe.

This connection with nature feeds the spirit and connects us both to our Child selves and to our ancestors. In the ancient world people believed that the so-called inanimate world of plants, stones, air, fire and water was inhabited by spirits. This is evident in the myths of the classical world, in Norse legends and Celtic lore. These beliefs persist to this day in Druidic practices, the Native American way of life and many other indigenous cultures worldwide.

Jan recognised that she seemed to have tapped into this tradition as a child on holiday in a remote country place:

> "I'd sneak out before sunrise and climb up the hill. I'd pick blackberries and mushrooms for breakfast, but that was mainly to have something to show for where I'd been. I really went for the rituals. I'd collect sticks and take them home to whittle and polish. Then I'd go up there and make patterns with stones and the whittled sticks.
>
> "I don't know why I practised these rituals, and I don't think I knew then. I just needed to do it; it was natural and necessary. I was also fascinated by the woman who appeared regularly on the opposite headland, moving in a ritual dance and flinging up her arms to the sky. The adults called her the mad woman, and I was warned against walking up there. I guess she was a kindred spirit, but I didn't know it then."

In adults the strength of the yearning to make a connection with nature still persists. I was drawn back to childhood roots in middle age. I returned to live in the place where I'd experienced a golden age of childhood when I was nine or ten. I found that walking the streets and lanes and hillsides that I walked as a child reactivated knowledge that had been lost for years. In particular, as I walked between deep Devon banks in Spring, I started recognising the wild flowers that were so much part of my life back then. Every morning a new species would have sprung open. As I saw it my heart would leap towards it with the memory of the same flower growing out of the wall on my route to school, or flourishing in the woods where we used to picnic. A whole world of smells and voices would overwhelm me at the sight of a tiny flower. The names of some came to me instantly and unexpectedly. Others surfaced two or three mornings later. I'd get a mental image of my nature diary with its marbled brown, stiff cover and the careful paintings of flowers and birds labelled with neatly joined-up writing.

We also see this yearning in the following descriptions taken from a book about women gardeners. Countess and author Elizabeth von Arnim was a woman of leisure and standing, who was expected to engage in feminine pursuits indoors but who clearly longed to get soil under her finger nails. No doubt many women forced by poverty to labour in the fields would have willingly changed places with the countess, but there are also many who would not exchange the outdoor life for any amount of comfort indoors. She writes in 1897:

> "I sometimes literally ache with envy as I watch the men going about their pleasant work in the sunshine, turning up the luscious damp earth ... [every]thing that they do ... fills my soul with longing to be up and doing too."[4]

In the following spring her aching to grow morning glories was such that, in the gardener's dinner hour, she did:

> "slink out with a spade and a rake and feverishly dig a piece of ground ... and sow surreptitious ipomaea and run back very hot and guilty into the house and get into a chair and behind a book and look languid just in time to save my reputation."[5]

NATURE AS METAPHOR

Today women rarely have the leisure or the need to look languid, but still the longing to connect to the natural world is unexpectedly close to the surface. This was demonstrated to me one day when I was working with a group of mature students, both women and men, in high stress jobs. Most were doubtful to the point of cynicism about the possibility or value of allowing themselves reflective space. But one of them commented that he had the advantage of working in a rural location. He would always find time to stop the car for fifteen minutes to reflect between appointments.

> "Gazing at the landscape and the weather helps me to stay sane. I find a lay-by and stop to clear my mind. It's never very long but it makes all the difference."

The group agreed guardedly to my suggestion that they use the lunch break to take a walk and clear their minds. I asked them to find a natural object which expressed something of what they were feeling about their work. I was doubtful that the more cynical members would respond to this invitation but, without exception, they brought pieces of the natural world back into the room and each was eloquent in describing what they represented.

Gareth held up a single blade of grass, saying:

> "I always get cut back, mown down. It represents the futility of my attempts to make a difference and grow. Yes, OK, the grass always grows back, but what's the point?"

Dawn dumped a large stone on the table showing how weighed down she felt by her responsibilities, and Richard presented a frond of rowan leaves with a cluster of scarlet berries:

> "I do a lot of hill climbing. I've always identified with the rowan tree. It grows in such unexpected places, all barren rocks and then you see this."

The group found that the natural objects they collected led into the world of metaphor. This gave them fresh insight into their dilemmas and unlocked their creativity amidst a great deal of laughter. One of them described this route through metaphor as *"opening a window in the gloom of the impossible."*

The theme of keeping hope alive in adverse circumstances is echoed in the following personal anecdote.

A friend of mine sent her granddaughters an Easter parcel with a difference. She found two beribboned Easter bonnets and filled them with packets of seeds – sunflowers, mustard and cress – that would give a fast or dramatic return for effort. She added some cream eggs and lollipops, but her signature as a gardener was in the seeds. She was acting with intent and told me a story about her father, who had grown up in an end of terrace back-to-back in Leeds. As his parents were coal merchants, there was a yard for the horses and the coal chute. A major memorable event of his childhood had been sowing some grass seed in the coal dust along the edge of the chute and watching it grow. It must have seemed like a miracle to see the black dust turning green. We were having this conversation on Easter Sunday 2003, just after the war against Iraq, and her father had reflected that if Saddam Hussein had been given grass seed to grow, the war might not have happened. This comment may make a number of assumptions and beg some tricky questions, but it is not a simplistic remark. There is a wealth of detail and complication that accompanies a child being given grass seed to grow. It reaches back into the attitudes of the previous generation and it assumes the love and patience that nurtures that seed into the future. Regardless of Saddam Hussein, I learned a valuable lesson in grandmotherliness that Easter Day. My friend's father, Jimmy Newell, is now well into his ninety-first year and still gardening. Thank you, Jimmy.

When I meet with groups of women to explore women's ways of knowing, I ask them to bring with them a natural object that is important to them. We spend some time telling the stories of these objects and what messages they bring to their finders. For example, Elaine brought a spray of sweet chestnut, the nuts cased in bright green, soft, yet spiny covers. She said, "this reminds me that sometimes I need to protect myself, but that the protection need not be hard. And I can still stay a rich, warm colour inside." I am always moved to hear how each woman's object came to her and how she found her spiritual home, whether in the woods or by the sea, in a park or in her back garden. So your next task is to commune with a natural object that is special to you.

EXERCISE - TUNING INTO AN OBJECT

First find a natural object that is special to you.

Arrange to have about half an hour of uninterrupted time. Place drawing materials to hand and make the usual preparations.

Hold your object or have it in front of you if it is too large or too delicate to hold.

Relax by breathing deeply several times and contracting and letting go of muscles throughout your body. Start with your feet and work up through your body until your whole system feels stretched and relaxed.

Take your attention into the object. Notice its texture and the energy you feel from it.

Remember or imagine where it came from before it came to you.

Is it part of something larger? How will it have changed in the course of its existence?

Follow its life back to its origins. Don't think too hard, allow your intuition to lead you.

During that process notice the effect of the seasons.

What happens to it at night?

Is your object affected by the weather? By sunshine, rain, wind or cold?

> As you track back to its origins, notice its relationship to other natural objects.
>
> When you reach its 'birth' or what feels like its origins, track forward again to the time you found it.
>
> Notice any message it has for you. Ask it what it wants to tell you. This may not be conveyed in words, but as an image or feeling.
>
> Thank your object.
>
> When you are ready, open your eyes and take some time to draw any image that came to you, or to write down a message that you received.

PARTICIPATION

Donna Ladkin comments that we need not be surprised at the resonance we feel with the natural world:

> *"Modern cosmology tells us that we come from the stars. That the same material that is in our bodies has existed in the universe since the initial Big Bang."* [6]

Donna remembers walking in the woods with her grandfather and how the earth *"seemed to communicate with him through the soles of his feet."* [7] She describes the exchange that appeared to take place:

> *"It was as if his city persona seeped down his body, drained out of his feet, and let something else back up, something that gave his gait a gentle bounce. It seemed like the woods were cleaning him out ..."* [8]

This resonates with Anita's experience:

> *"The sea or the woods are places I go to meet myself. I can just be. And my real self comes to the surface and I begin to know where I am. It slows me down. And it's like it cleanses me. I feel washed through by the sound of the waves or the wind in the trees, or by the green light filtering through a canopy of leaves."*

These are ways into 'participation' with the natural world, a word that is much used in writing about ecology and environmental issues. What does it mean? Donna Ladkin suggests that participation is *"rooted in communication"*. She considers that we have *"forgotten the 'language of the trees', and with practice can return to our birthright of full participation with the cosmos."*[9]

Clarissa Pinkola Estés says something very similar when she refers to the wildish intuitive powers of women which *"become as buried streams within women, buried by disrepute and disuse,"* and which can again become *"fully manifested"* with exercise.[10] We can engage in practices that bring this connection more readily and more often into awareness. Indeed we need constant reminders as a counterbalance to our cultural conditioning that makes it difficult for us to see the inter-relatedness of all things. When we feel we belong in the natural world and communicate with it as readily as we pick up the phone to talk to a best friend, then maybe we are truly participating.

The natural world is always there. All we have to do is connect with it, rest in it, listen to it, ask for help and be healed. It is important to have a place where you can do this, and it is best to have a real as well as an imaginary place to visit. In that place you can begin or continue to develop your relationship with nature. You can relax and be. You can observe minutely and you can also gaze and absorb without consciously looking.

EXERCISE - FINDING A PLACE

Give yourself an hour or so to go for a walk in the countryside. Choose a location that you feel particularly drawn to. Ideally this will be a place you can visit easily and frequently, so you may want to choose part of your garden or a park. If it has to be at a distance it will be possible to visit in your imagination when you are unable to travel there in person.

Walk with a relaxed attention. Your aim is to find a place where you can be undisturbed. Hold that aim lightly and trust that it will work out. Your purpose is to go with the flow of your intuition rather than to have a fixed goal in mind.

If you feel drawn to a particular clump of trees or boulder, follow that impulse. Walk around any area that seems possible. Touch the trees or rocks or earth. Ask whether they welcome you there. Check your body sensations to know whether this place feels right for you.

If it does, settle there for a time and get to know it with all your senses. Feel the support that it gives to your body. Notice the shapes, movements and colours all around you. Listen to the noises, starting with the furthest sound you can hear and bringing your attention nearer and nearer. Explore the environment with your fingers and your sense of smell.

When you feel complete, thank the spirit of the place and leave, taking note of how you came there and how you will find it again.

Don't worry if you don't find a "right spot" at your first attempt. Try again on another occasion. It took me several months, and two intermediate places, before I found one where I felt truly at home. Sooner or later your place will make itself known.

> Follow your intuition too if you feel frightened or anxious, and leave the place. This is not an endurance test. Nor is it wise to put yourself at risk. Maybe you would feel safer in a park than in the wild. Or maybe a trusted friend could accompany you and stay in the vicinity.
>
> Once you have found your special place it will always be there to visit, whether in body or in imagination.

If we spend time regularly 'being' in such a place we come to know that the interconnectedness of all things is not an intellectual invention. If we observe closely and openly for long enough, it becomes clear. Professor Peter Reason of Bath University points this out. It is not about being *"nice and kind to the environment"* for *we are* 'the environment':

"Our relationship to the Earth is that of a leaf to a tree. We have no independent existence. No tree, no leaf." [11]

Peter experienced this as he watched earth and trees in a woodland and became aware also of invisible bacteria, elements and molecules. He realised *"that everything I could see and imagine was in the process of becoming something else, that everything was participating in everything else."*

The art of Andy Goldsworthy [12] captures this working of one element on another. In the first stage of creation he works hard, often against time, and aiming for perfection, to create a form using one element, while the next stages consist of other elements transforming and eventually obliterating his work. The tide washes over a sand sculpture and sweeps it away. The wind blows a sand carving off the trunk of a tree. An artifact of ice, created in freezing conditions overnight, melts when the sun comes up. A river carries a spiral of sticks or a snake of leaves downstream and out to sea. His works are acts of participation with the elements, seasons and the climate. The weather conditions, the time of day and the work of the elements are included in his description and part of the co-created art.

The landscape painter, Sarah Gillespie, conjures up the elements and wilderness in quite a different process of participation. Sarah paints land and seascapes but she is not what I would call a representational artist. In an exhibition brochure her works are described as representational, but a paradox is involved; *"We must reassess what they represent."*[13] She explained how she works from natural objects, but doesn't actually represent them in her art. *"I might start from a moth's wing, but the inspiration is qualitative rather than direct or specific."* When I produced a stone from my pocket she pointed out the similar tonality of the red of the stone and the cream of the stripe across it, as well as the fineness of the line. *"People have painted stones and enlarged them, that's been done. I'd work from the fineness of that line and the colours and capture the quality of the stone when painting something quite other."* Sarah is looking beyond the surface and representing the underlying structure, the connecting patterns found throughout nature. That is what makes her work 'representational' at a deep, rather than a surface, level. So it is not surprising if people experience a sense of connection with the natural world when they encounter Sarah's work. But this is not her experience of creating it. For her, this interpretation misses the point of what motivates her as an artist: *"What drives me in my painting is the pain of being separate – from nature, from each other, from the divine, or whatever you want to call it."*

This pain of separation can be a symptom of many different kinds of loss: loss of identity; loss of a human mother, loss of connection with Mother Earth or loss of our 'goddess' energy. And it is the same pain that people daily try to anaesthetise with drugs, alcohol, sex, busy-ness and any number of forms of denial.

Anita had a powerful experience of participation during a group meeting. The discussion revolved around the destruction of ancient civilisations which honoured and worshipped the earth and the whole natural world:

> "It was relevant that my back and neck had been manipulated the day before. The manipulation had been difficult and dramatic, and it had left me with strange, spaced-out sensations afterwards. But it really freed me up. The image I had of my back while sitting in the group was of something newly free and supple, but also soft and vulnerable. I was concerned to keep it supple, but also to protect it. It felt very vulnerable. I felt a bit like a snail or a tortoise without its shell."

Anita linked this to what had happened on the way to the meeting:

> "While driving, suddenly my perspective flipped from seeing the view ahead as a road to drive along, to seeing it as earth covered in a tarmac crust. For a short moment I was more aware of the underlying earth I couldn't see, than the surface tarmac of the everyday road. And in that perception I identified with the earth, and experienced the tarmac as horribly irksome and oppressive, stifling really.
>
> "And this image, this sensation came back to me during the discussion. I was feeling the pain of the earth, and tears started to well up and silently overflow. It was like some sort of independent force or process, which just happened to be taking place in my body. It seemed that my physical state, the image I had seen, and the theme of the meeting combined to allow the tears to flow. I felt that they were my contribution to the discussion."

If we are free to spend time in the wild, participation can turn into an ongoing dialogue with nature.

For Sadie, an American who regularly summers in a primitive log cabin by a lake, participation meant immersing herself in the water and sharing her space with wild creatures who were often her only companions. She rose with the sun and dipped into the lake every morning to swim:

> *"A wonderful treat, silent mist cloaking the surface of the water. Ten minutes later the lake was shrouded completely in mist as if it wasn't ready yet to engage with the heat of the day."*

She wakes to a chorus of chickadees and bathes with a group of loons (diving birds with black and white spotted feathers) who come for "early morning socialising". When a friend set rat traps to catch a thieving squirrel, Sadie noticed that the squirrel simply left the camp, returning when the friend had left and Sadie had removed the traps.

THE ELEMENTS

To begin to understand this connectedness with nature, we need to spend time 'hanging out' in the natural world and discovering the healing that this brings. One way of approaching this is to consider the four main elements of Earth, Air, Fire and Water. You will probably find that one of the elements appeals to you more than the others and that is a good place to start. It is of course almost impossible to engage with each element entirely in isolation. In nature they are always combined and their dynamic interaction draws us into their dance and has a powerful effect on the human soul. But to get to know them better, try narrowing your focus onto one at a time.

WATER

Water is the element that we all come from. I can sit and watch the sea breaking over a rock for hours at a time and my emotional and spiritual health has always depended on regular visits to the sea. When people come to stay with us, especially if they are city dwellers, the first thing they want to do is go to the sea, whatever the weather.

If your special element is water, try noticing at a mundane level how much and how often we use it during a day. Washing, cleaning our teeth, flushing the toilet, having a coffee: our society benefits from an abundance of water piped for our convenience. The least we can do is appreciate it as it flows through our hands. If the weather has been dry, rain comes as a relief. Walk out in it and enjoy the feel of it on your skin. Notice the pattern it makes on dry earth and paving stones. If you live in a wet climate, notice how many kinds of rain there are, from soft mist to torrential downpour. Watch how it changes the light; listen to it gurgling in gutters and gullies; smell the freshness of damp earth and wet grass after a shower. Seek out water to soothe your mood and heal stress. To calm your nerves in the city, sit and watch a fountain in a park, or fish swimming in an aquarium. If you are angry, shouting your rage into a rough sea is wonderful therapy. The waves, or a flowing river, will wash away thoughts and feelings that you need to let go.

People who live near water quickly learn to respect this element. Storms, high tides, strong currents and swollen rivers take their toll every year and the fishing industry is one of the most dangerous in terms of lives lost at sea.

But whether the ocean is wild or calm, it widens our perspective. It has a quality that dissolves our confusions and bad tempers and lets our grief flow. We listened to the sounds of water in the womb and it still soothes us as adults, while drinking water cleanses the body of toxins. It is exhilarating to dance naked in the deluge that breaks a period of sultry heat in the summer; to feel the rain stinging your face on a winter walk; or to dip your hot feet in a cold mountain stream on a hill climb. Equally, water energy can be calming, teaching us to go with the flow and to be persistent, for it is the gentle force that wears away the stone.

EARTH

The element Earth encompasses so much. It is the land, the foundation on which we walk, the soil that grows our food. And it is the rocks and minerals inside the earth and the plants that grow out of it. The energy of Earth gives us a solid and practical foundation and 'keeps our feet on the ground'. Too much earthy energy and we become rooted to the spot with 'feet of clay' and overwhelmed, as if buried under the weight of a landslide of mud.

If your strong element is earth, then you probably like gardening and going barefoot in summer. To build that up, attend to becoming more aware of the seasons, pushing plants into the earth with your fingers, making compost and noticing the cycle of decay and renewal. A friend of mine insisted on taking her whole family camping every August so that she could feel her feet on the earth all the time. Maybe you don't feel equal to camping, but try leaning against a tree and resting in its protection. Walk barefoot on rocks, grass or sand. If you wear shoes you don't notice how different the grass or sand feels in the dewy morning and in the sun-baked middle of the day. Lie on the ground on your back and feel the earth holding you under the arch of the sky. Roll over and watch insects burrowing through grass as you listen to the heartbeat of the earth. Jan describes how she feels supported by the earth:

> "I feel held by the earth, I really do. I had a fall once, quite a long fall from a footpath and when I landed I was lying there in shock and it came to me. The earth would always hold me. That I couldn't fall off. It's obvious of course, but it was immensely comforting. I wrote a poem about it."

Plants are also of the earth, and wise women for centuries have learned the wisdom of using their subtle powers for nourishment and healing. For an understanding of how this ancient tradition sits in the context of modern and complementary medicine, read Susun Weed [14], who shows the way to trusting our inner knowing.

FIRE

The element Fire gives us warmth and passion and its natural source is the sun. It is easy to see the fire element as destructive when house fires kill families, and bush fires or volcanic lava wipe out whole areas of land and settlement. Similarly Fire energy in humans can manifest in violence and road rage. But Fire also gives us creative, sexual energy that we may take into any area of our lives, including relationships. It gives us zest for life, outrage at injustice and the passion to make changes.

If it is your key element, then you will probably find long, wet winters depressing. So make sure you have a source of fire, best of all logs on the hearth or a wood-burning stove. On one misjudged holiday in a wet November in Wales, I spent a great deal of time drinking tea in the nearby café in order to soak up the energy of their roaring fire. Our cottage was centrally heated and warm but I could get no comfort from the glowing imitation coals in the fireplace.

Other sources of warmth are spicy foods and teas. Use seasonal root vegetables in casseroles and roasts in winter to feed your fire. Surround yourself in a cocoon of rich, warm colours and fabrics in furnishings and clothes. Take the opportunity to bask in the sun when it is out and let it soak into your bones. Go out early to greet the sun and, as you watch it break over the horizon, give thanks for the return of its warmth after the cold night.

AIR

To connect to Air energy go walking and feel the wind in your hair on a hilltop. Autumn is a good time for walking in the woods and seeing the leaves whirling earthwards on currents of air. A simple and obvious way to attune to Air energy is to focus on your breathing, noticing how deep or shallow it is, how fast or slow. When we stand still too long or get in a rut, then we need a 'breath of fresh air' or the 'winds of change' to move us on. We see the extreme of that in nature in the hurricanes and tornados that destroy everything in their path and leave people no alternative but to start again from nothing. This may be the origin of the metaphor 'to throw everything up in the air' when we have need of a fresh perspective on a problem. Air is essentially about communication so it also embraces language and ideas, poetry and the tradition of story-telling. Singing, laughing and playing music are expressions of Air energy, as well as dance and movement. We see the negative side of that in 'hot air' and confusion when we are 'blown in all directions' by conflicting forces, or bored and baffled by obscure or pompous language.

CITY DWELLING

If you live in a city it may be more difficult to make these connections. In urban environments we tend to experience the elements as getting in the way. Natural disasters like earthquakes and hurricanes have worse consequences in a city where toppled buildings compound the danger. At a more mundane level, compare the frustrations of fighting through a downpour in the city when you are smartly dressed and battling with an umbrella, to a rainstorm in the country when you are out with the dog in a waterproof and gumboots.

So do the best you can with what you have. To feel better about Water in the city, put your boots on when it rains, splash through the puddles in the park and notice how much the ducks are enjoying it. If your town is on a tidal river like the Thames, notice the state of the tide as you cross the bridge on your way to work. Keep track of the phases of the moon. Think of your shower as a waterfall, or run a deep bath and imagine yourself immersed in the ocean. The energy of water is flowing, reflective and emotional, so you might write a journal of your emotional state, or better still paint those feelings in water colours. To tune into watery energy choose blue and aqua and green in fabrics that drape and flow. A fish tank can be more restful to watch than the television, and a water feature in a courtyard may be as soothing as a stream flowing over rocks.

To connect with Earth, explore the parks and take notice of how your favourite trees change with the seasons. Try going out early to listen to the birds, and bring natural objects likes twigs and stones and autumn leaves into your home. When you do this, make it a rule not to break pieces off a plant or a larger rock. Remember that this world is not inanimate as we have been taught. If ever you need to pick anything, silently ask permission and only take it if you sense that the answer is yes. At home you can sow seeds in a window box and talk to your house plants. Lyall Watson [15] in his book Supernature records the reaction of a plant to stress and to careful treatment. The plant not only registered distress at the experimenter's *thought* of burning one of its leaves, but also at the death of shrimps dropped into boiling water in the same room.

The Fire element in the form of something actually burning will be hard to come by in a city flat if you haven't the advantage of an open grate or a stove. So play with other sources of light and with the creative energy of fire. Candles are a source of natural light. Combine them with other soft lighting, rich colours and reflective materials to give warmth to a room. Remember that warming foods and drinks also feed the fire element. Find an outlet to transform aggressive fire energy into passion and creativity. You might channel it into a cause, or into a craft or skill like raku-fired clay work, cookery or martial arts. Above all, make an effort to slow down and let go of the busy agenda in order to avoid 'burn-out'. There is always a reason behind a name.

Air is a difficult element for the town dweller if we attend solely to the fresh variety. City air conjures up exhaust fumes and the stale, hot winds of underground railways. Sleeping with a window open may be a security risk, may be noisy and may let in more carbon monoxide than fresh air. Walk in the park on a windy day and watch the clouds racing and the birds swooping on the air currents. And for unpolluted air go to the country or the seaside at the weekend. Alternatively focus on the energy of Air. Using incense sticks and hanging a string of downy feathers or wind chimes near the window gives a sense of airiness. (Don't do as I did and hang them outside, where they sounded like an ice-cream van in a strong wind and drove the neighbours crazy.)

Anything that moves the atmosphere through resonance or vibration brings the energy of air into your living space. Sweep away stagnation by clearing clutter and cleaning regularly and reward yourself by singing and dancing to music while you do it. Then put your feet up, admire the effects of your labours and read some poetry out loud to yourself.

EXERCISE - EXPLORING THE ELEMENTS

Prepare drawing and painting materials, sugar paper, scissors and a light glue or paste suitable for sticking paper.

The aim of this exercise is to make a collage or painting (or a combination) of each element – a representation without words.

I suggest that you take one element at a time.

First, make the usual preparations to become present in your body.

Go mentally or physically to your special place. Relax and tune in for 5 to 10 minutes to the element you have chosen. Ask what this element means to you and let your imagination take you where it will.

Next spend some time collecting ingredients that represent the quality of the element to you. You might want to do this outdoors or to trawl the house – your sewing basket, dried food jars, jewellery box, d.i.y. cupboard and magazines are all potential sources.

Finally, spend a happy hour assembling your work of art and finding a place to display your gallery of pictures.

Repeat this process for each of the elements in your own time.

IN OUR OWN TIME

You may notice that immersing yourself in the elements in this way changes your perceptions so that time does indeed become your own. It is as if the passage of time slows down or becomes unimportant. In the natural world time is measured by the passage of the sun across the sky, the cycles of the moon and the rotating seasons. The artificial system that humans have invented has no meaning in nature, but it takes an effort to let go of our reliance on it. For this reason, when Sadie arrives at her cabin in the wilds, she takes off her watch and only puts it on again when she leaves. However, not everyone chooses to set aside living by the measurement of hours, minutes and seconds and one of Sadie's visitors routinely winds up her clock on arrival. And she in turn stops it again when he leaves. For her, the light and the promptings of her own body provide sufficient structure for her days.

For Anna Lea Merritt, a gardener and painter writing in 1908, becoming absorbed in the elements can be deeply relaxing to the psyche. For her, a nine-hour day weeding in the rain is preferable to a rest cure:

> *"A really long day of weeding is a restful experience, and quite changes the current of thought. ... After such a day my fingers are bleeding, knees tottering, back bent, dress muddy and soaking ... but I have attained the most profound inward peace ..."* [16]

Judith Duerk describes reaching a similar spiritual state through a process also involving hard physical work and lasting several days. She sets out to clear a pile of twigs and brushwood, starting out *"with a vengeance"* but getting nowhere with her *"petulant rippings and tearings"*. Slowing down and working more methodically allows a quieter rhythm to emerge. By the second day she has stopped viewing the task as a means to an end (of clearing a space in which to write) and is absorbed in the task for its own sake. She finds herself writing when she rests, and on the third day she becomes aware of *"something wondrous happening"*:

"My whole experience was shifting ... the molecules of time, itself, opened up before me, ... A hush was in the woods around, as well as deep within me ... it was as if I had slipped through a scrim into a timeless, mysterious realm ... silent ... shimmering with life." [17]

Duerk distinguishes between *ordinary Chronos* time, which we use every day, and *sacred Kairos* time of the feminine realm, which she experienced in the woods. She reflects upon the compression of time in modern life and fears for women existing with only a linear awareness of time:

"... for her sense of sacred Kairos time is the precious essence of life. There must be time enough for her to experience the sacredness within each moment and within herself." [18]

NATURE AND THE SACRED

Anita had such a shift of perception standing on a headland:

"I was suddenly aware of the ground under my feet sliding into the water and extending under the ocean to emerge as another land mass. My senses ballooned to encompass both the headland and the whole earth. It gave me a sense of the planet as a whole with myself as part of it, at once infinitely small but also immensely important because I had a place in the pattern of all life."

We see the erosion of rocks, the leaves falling in autumn, the process of decay in the woods and in our gardens, and we see new life pushing through the earth and bursting from branches in spring. The cycles and inter-relationships that we cannot see are even more complex. The atmosphere regulates itself by a series of chemical and physical checks and balances, a system that embraces all of life in *"an intricate, self-sustaining and self-organising web."* [19]

We humans are part of that system. By immersing ourselves in the elements we become aware of that connection and can let go of the tension of 'keeping the elements at bay' that tends to dominate our lives in urban and suburban environments. As I walk on the beach I notice Water and Air combining to make swirls and spirals in the sand at the foot of a rock. This microcosmic world is contained by Earth, while the play of light reveals it and draws it to the attention. Without Fire there would be no light, and Water and Fire are both necessary to the growth of plants, which in turn change the chemical balance of Air. The presence or absence of Fire produces hot springs or icebergs. And although Fire can make water boil, Water can also douse fire, which cannot burn without Air.

This immersion allows us to become less brittle, to soften and relax and to be open to shifts of consciousness.

Nina describes this process of letting go:

> "When I go out into nature everything inside me seems to change. I feel different. Life doesn't seem to be so difficult anymore. I slow down inside and start to breathe again. I feel part of something bigger and somehow even death doesn't appear to be so frightening anymore. I have always felt that I would like to be out in nature when I die - where dying is just a matter of course - another part of the cycle of things. It holds a perspective for me where nothing else does, life and the natural way of things, and that is a great comfort to me. It also reminds me of just how little control I do have in life."

Giving up control is not always easy.

For Sadie, spending a month in her wilderness camp in Vermont means confronting solitude as well as the challenge of the wild with no plumbing or electricity. She starts out feeling "terrified and unsettled". After a day she records:

> "Skies cleared after lunch yesterday to a beautiful evening and gentle sunset. My spirits and confidence improved as if with the weather but, it seems, also with "doing it". If you don't attend to practical matters in this environment it all falls apart. Anxiety noticeably down as I found solutions to potential problems. I managed the keel-less canoe alone by weighting the bow with a bucket of water and stones. I solved the problem of algae in the spring by bailing ferociously, and managed to haul a new gas tank into camp without wrecking my back. And I picked a fresh bouquet of Michaelmas daisies! That was as important as the other tasks. Then I had an idyllically beautiful meal last night, at sunset. Full moon shining into my bedroom and glistening at 1.00am ... alone."

But on the third day her anxiety is persisting:

> "Beautiful sunrise, clear sky, sun dappling through the maple and birch leaves. Yesterday's sun and fresh SW breeze helped me to settle and relax, but I am still anxious at the core. Finding it difficult to feel totally calm and as if I am in the right place ... feels like I am waiting, expectant."

Sadie's reward for staying with her vulnerable, open state is a vision or dream on the fourth morning:

> "I found an image hanging in front of my eyes as I woke. It was detailed and clear and eighteen inches away, a gift."

It seems that being alone in Nature has opened up a channel. Sadie feels that the message is coming from another part of herself, "another dimension of my being," bestowing an image which represents the universe and her place in it. She is able to take this metaphor away and use it as a source of guidance which has a lasting effect:

> "I have been aware of a shift in my awareness, my peripheral vision has expanded. I notice the weather, the wind, light and the moods of the land in a way that I hadn't before. It is in my line of sight rather than providing

the backcloth to personal interactions. I had allowed people in my personal and professional world to crowd it out. Health and balance returns ..."

How important it is to have that solitary connection with the natural world. To achieve that solitude, free from others, Elizabeth von Arnim creeps out of her house at three in the morning and is well rewarded:

> "There in front of me was the sundial ... but how strange and unfamiliar it all looked, and how holy – as though God must be walking there in the cool of the day. ... and everywhere there was the same mystery, and emptiness, and wonder." [20]

This sense of mystery and wonder is echoed in the following experience described by Fritjof Capra. Capra was sitting watching the ocean when he experienced at first hand the structure of matter as a *"gigantic cosmic dance"*. From his work as a physicist he knew that the environment consisted of vibrating molecules and atoms. It was as if familiar diagrams came to life:

> "I 'saw' cascades of energy coming down from outer space, in which particles were created and destroyed in rhythmic pulses; I 'saw' the atoms of the elements and those of my body participating in this cosmic dance of energy; I felt its rhythm and I 'heard' its sound ..." [21]

It reminds me of the way the ocean shimmers with light in a Gillespie painting. For me, she has captured this cosmic dance and that is why her work sends shivers down my spine. Leslie Kenton describes a similar epiphany in her young life when she was 18 years old, in love, and walking in Golden Gate Park.

> "Space expanded in all directions. A million tiny holes appeared in reality – each emitting light – so that the air and grass, the pavement ... the clouds ... the trees ... trembled with radiance. Time burst wide open to break in great waves over the lawn. My heart seemed to grow to immense proportions." [22]

She found the experience both *"joyous and terrifying"* and she resolved to live more at that level of being. How might we all do that?

MAKING OUR CONNECTION

Throughout this chapter we have been contemplating a view of the world which is almost certainly different from the one that most of us grew up with. The prevalent view for centuries has been that the natural world is a non-intelligent resource at the disposal of rational human beings, who have concentrated their efforts on controlling and exploiting that resource. However, we have been exploring the idea that the universe is an interconnected system that includes human beings as one of its parts. Along with rocks and trees, animals and rivers, we are all part of the web of life. What we do affects all parts of the web. We have also seen that the non-human part of that world can be a source of wisdom for us.

How do we get used to this approach and how do we use the understanding that we have gained? At one level we may have always understood the world in this way, our inner Child carrying that knowledge for us. But at another we are inevitably influenced by the conventional view, as well as seduced by the social patterns and industries that depend upon that view. In the 20th century it became obvious that the behaviour of human beings was severely damaging the rest of the system. But, because we have so much invested in the conventional view - socially, psychologically and financially - the destructive behaviour persists. Even those who are ready to embrace the new ideas at an intellectual level find it is much harder to change their hearts and behaviour. That can only flow from a deep sense of identity with the whole system.

At this point I could exhort you to recycle and join campaigns to save the world. But it would be more fitting for this journey to take a more organic and feminine approach. Ask yourself what is right for you. That might be any of a range of things from joining a political party with a strong environmental agenda, to sitting with your back against a tree *"listening to the wind"* [17], and everything in between. But start small. Start inside. Start by tuning in to your inner wisdom, your elemental knowing. Go out into the natural world and invoke its power to help you in this. Answers always seem forthcoming if we only ask. They come in a variety of ways: sometimes arising instantly and surprisingly; sometimes later in the form of a letter or phone call; sometimes in the pattern of events that unfold in the weeks that follow the question.

This is by no means to underestimate the importance of measures at local, national and international level to address the ecological crisis we have reached. But at a personal level the *Why* and the *How* of what we are doing is as important as *What* we choose to do. If we merely respond to external imperatives, it is difficult to sustain a commitment to doing what they ask of us.

Take slimming, for example. If we aim to lose weight and discipline our bodies with every new diet and an attitude of deprivation or self-righteousness, it tends not to last beyond the novelty of each regime. If we start from a position of respecting our body, wanting our system to be clean and healthy, wanting to have more energy and move more easily, we are more likely to succeed. Our body will then tell us how to regulate our eating and drinking patterns over time with more enduring results. It is the same with ecology.

Maybe we start by balancing economy with appreciation of the resources that we use. For instance, savour the shower water sluicing over your body, wallow in the bath. But turn off the tap while you brush your teeth and get leaky washers fixed promptly. Don't stint on lighting your home well, but use long life bulbs and take more care to turn off lights in empty rooms. Try driving more slowly, especially in the early morning when the temptation is to take advantage of the empty roads and make up time. For this is the time when vulnerable small creatures are more likely to be venturing onto the tarmac.

My reward one morning was meeting a hare. I dropped back, dipped the headlights and was able to watch it loping ahead of me until it danced sideways into a gateway.

EXERCISE - WAYS OF PARTICIPATING

Visit your special place, either physically or mentally.

Relax your body in the usual way and ask the question:
"How should I participate with the natural world?"

Let the answer come – or not! Don't try too hard and don't worry if no answer seems to come. Trust that you will receive the message that is right for you in a way that is fitting.

Be aware that the answer may come in a variety of ways. It may come in an image, with a falling leaf or a flitting bird, in a phrase that floats into your mind or a happening that occurs after you have stopped looking out for it.

You may get a "big picture" answer or one that indicates a small and precise action. Either way, this is a question that you can revisit as often as it feels relevant as your relationship with the natural world develops and changes.

What would your Wise Woman do?

She'd step out on the earth, feel the sun, wind and rain on her skin.

Then she would know what to do.

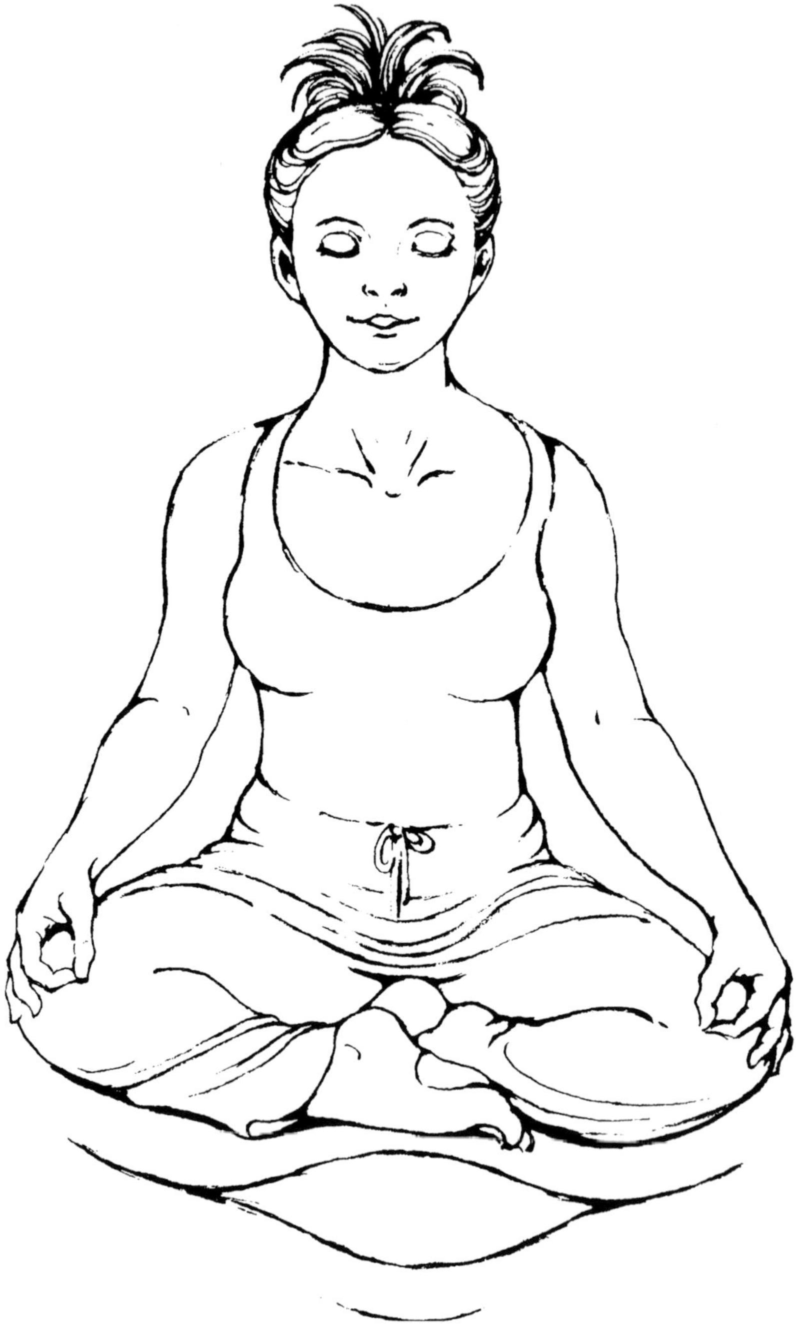

– CHAPTER 11 –
THE SILENCE OF WOMEN

"The sound of silence breaking makes us understand what we could not hear before ... listen very carefully to the language of silence ... for women come from such a long silence."
Sheila Rowbotham [1]

"The world is divided into *'teapot'* and *'mountain'* people," said Margaret during a consultancy session. She identified teapots as artifacts, practical objects with a specific use, and teapot activity was therefore essentially task-focused and purposeful. Mountains on the other hand are natural and have no practical use. They just are. So mountain behaviour is the ability simply to be. Both these behaviours have their place. Taken to extremes, teapot behaviour can become 'busy-busy' or ineffective fire-fighting; and mountain behaviour can spiral off into unrealistic fantasy or endless meditation. As emphasised previously, we need a balance of action and reflection, and the ability to 'teapot' or 'mountain' as appropriate. Usually in our culture, the pressures of our fast-paced lives lead us to neglect mountain behaviour. We need the creative kind of silence symbolised by mountains. But the long silence referred to above is of a very different kind. It is a constraining silence from which we need to break free.

What does it feel like inside this unwilling silence? There is no simple answer to this. It is complicated and difficult to analyse and varies from individual to individual. For example, when challenged in any situation by family members, friends or strangers, how often do we flounder and then think of a suitable response as we lie in bed that night? Whether the gap between challenge and response is ten minutes, twenty-four hours or ten days, our credibility, our very self-esteem depends on reducing it. There are variations on this theme.

Sometimes we know exactly what response to make but we don't trust ourselves, or we hold back for some other reason.

Sometimes we experience this gap as a straightforward delay in our thinking process, a lack of mental agility, and envy people who have the ability to think fast on their feet, and to interpret or make wise comments on what is happening in the moment. We experience some frustration and move on.

At other times we experience this gap as more than a delayed reaction. It can be disabling and all embracing, something that swallows us up and denies us access to our intuition as well.

Anita described this as feeling cut off, unable to know or be known, in a kind of paralysis:

> *"It was as if I was looking at myself through the wrong end of a telescope. I felt dissociated from what I was hearing and saying. It was as if I was in a glass box, cut off from directly engaging with the world. I would come over paralysed so that I couldn't think or speak. It was always worst whenever I thought other people had expectations of me. Not only could I not say what I wanted, but usually I didn't even know. If I did know, it seemed so 'wrong' that I'd have exploded rather than let it out."*

THE LANGUAGE OF SILENCE

Sheila Rowbotham[1] wrote back in the 1970s of listening to the *"language of silence"*. She found women *"mysteriously quiet"*, for when change is not conceived as remotely possible then there is no point in protesting. Clearly women have come a long way since then, but I still encounter plenty of women for whom this is still true. In October 2000 the glass ceiling was reported to be firmly in place in British business. In 10 top companies the number of women on the board had increased from a mere 2% to only 7% over ten years.[2] According to a survey by the Cranfield School of Management, the number of women directors in top companies fell for the third year running in 2001, only 57% having female directors compared with 64% in 1999.[3] Even among women who have succeeded and are accepted in what used to be men's worlds, there are signs that they do not share the values of the workaholic culture. Some who have reached the top are choosing to step down to enjoy life with their children. *"It did not seem important to jump the next hurdle in an impressively short time, or indeed at all,"* writes one.[4]

But the vast majority of women are not at the top and for many women these choices are still not real. Silent women do not make the headlines for obvious reasons. Many things contribute to this silence: fear of making fools of ourselves; avoidance of drawing attention to ourselves or attracting punishment; the need to be self-sufficient, to protect our children or to be loyal to a man; the horror of being a nuisance; or anxiety that our contribution will be inadequate. We hold back for fear of attracting criticism or starting an argument, to avoid winning or being more successful than others, or in order not to betray a confidence.

Of course this does not apply to all women. There are women everywhere who are successful, acute, argumentative, strident, diplomatic, burdensome, dependent, courageous, outspoken and so on. We are talking here about some women all of the time, many women some of the time, and even most women occasionally. Some apparently successful women, who clearly have a confident voice in the world, are silent about some part of their life and are less than they could be because of it. Often the part of their life that has fallen silent, or never found a voice is their inner wisdom. As Leslie Kenton puts it:

> *"A woman's creativity is stillborn. ... her soul has been silenced by her culture or by her own lack of self-belief."* [5]

There is as much reason to be concerned at the waste of this wisdom in a world that desperately needs it, as for the plight of women who are heavily oppressed by poverty or by constraining or violent relationships.

Women who are the victims of domestic violence are a prime example of those who find it difficult to break the habit of silence. Telling someone else of their predicament is a necessary first step in asserting themselves and doing something about it. A representative of a women's refuge referred in the year 2000 to the *"shame, secrecy and silence"* which characterises the experience and behaviour of victims of domestic violence. In spite of the fact that 1 in 4 women in the UK admitted to experiencing violence, it was estimated that only 2% of incidents were officially reported. In the port where she worked, of over 2,000 reported incidents, only 197 would go forward to prosecution. This widespread phenomenon is often due to the tendency of women to retreat into silence (sometimes under threat from their oppressors) after their first attempt at getting help.

Silence grows not only out of being violently abused but also out of not being understood, out of being laughed at, criticised or ignored. We are silent when we know our truth but don't know how to express it; when we want to hide our truth; and when we have been silent so long that we hardly recognise what we know or feel. Paul Newham, a voice and movement therapist, writes of voice as a political phenomenon. He has found that aphonia, or voice loss where there is no organic cause, is often a response to having one's right to a 'voice' denied.

> *"Aphonia represents the ultimate silence, and it frequently contains the only form of protest available to those who can withstand no more oppression."* [6]

90% of all such cases of psychosomatic voice loss he has encountered are women. Angela Carter[7] achieves a memorable portrayal of this condition in her novel *The Magic Toyshop*, in which the young heroine's Aunt Margaret is 'dumb', her silence a terrible affliction like a curse that came to her when she married tyrannical and violent Uncle Philip. He is described as liking his women silent and will not tolerate them wearing make-up or trousers. Her only jewellery apart from her wedding ring is a metal collar necklace, which is *"heavy, crippling and precious,"* in which she *"ate only with the utmost difficulty"* and which her husband had designed and made for her as a wedding present. In the cataclysmic finale of the book Aunt Margaret speaks again: *"Struck dumb on her wedding day, she found her old voice again on the day she was freed."*

Many women are silenced by the futility of attempting to communicate with partners.

Anita believed she was going mad because her perceptions of reality were so different from her husband's. It never occurred to her that she could be right instead of him, or that they could both be right:

> *"I got into a pattern. It was easier to be invisible and not to say what I thought or felt. I could hide that way. I didn't realise what I was doing to myself. I got into a powerless position just out of habit. Once I began to see that, it was like being suffocated and I needed to break out."*

So what is the language of silence? Let's explore some of its forms of expression.

TEARS

Most of us are familiar with the language and healing power of tears. The cool tears of grief wash our pain away. But the hot tears of anger are more complicated (especially when the two are intermingled). As described in a previous chapter, women often weep when they would prefer to rage, but convention still discourages it.

However, the tears that are the true language of silence often come unbidden, welling up to wet our cheeks unexpectedly when we detect no reason why we should be having such a reaction. Or they are shed in private, in the darkness of long nights without a witness.

They may not speak to others but they are an internal message that we should not ignore.

Clarissa Pinkola Estés reports that a woman's tears are considered dangerous because they *"loosen the locks and bolts on the secrets that she bears"*[8], the secrets of mothers, fathers, men and of women themselves. Tears may be dangerous to those involved in the secrets, but to women they are essential, for *"Weeping creates a river around the boat that carries your soul-life"*[8] and they are *"lenses through which we gain an alternative vision."*[9]

Think about your own tears. Do they flow easily? Too readily? Or are they locked up? What is their meaning and their message? For you? For others? Do you have someone who will be there for you when you need to cry?

LIES, SECRETS AND MANIPULATION

To some women lying becomes second nature. They lie to protect themselves, to please others and to be pleasing; to avoid an argument, criticism or disapproval; to gain power and control; to manipulate; to conceal feelings; to get their own way and out of habit.

Holding secrets is another form of lying that involves never being open or quite honest about the way things are. But secrets always find their way out. It may not happen directly in words but in one of the other idioms of the language of silence. This will happen however hard a woman tries to obey the injunction "don't tell!" The maintaining of lies and the keeping of secrets uses a lot of energy. It requires constant vigilance, attention to getting the story right and being consistent. *"A woman who carries a secret is an exhausted woman"* writes Estés.[10] She will be vulnerable to anything that will loosen her hold on these fictions, for the wise and silent woman deep inside her will be grateful to let them go.

It is hard to imagine the world without any form of manipulation. It would not necessarily be a better place. There are many forms of manipulative behaviour and it is not always easy to distinguish between them: criminal and moral blackmail; habitual or compulsive manipulation of people for selfish ends; the painstaking work of diplomacy; the tactful nudging of those we love; the skilful dance of bargaining and negotiation; and the playful manoeuvring of flirtation and courtship. The lines between destructive manipulation, wise strategy and harmless play are fine and difficult to draw. Different people would draw those lines in different places.

Take a piece of behaviour – it might for example involve you and another person, and you feel uncomfortable. One of you may be taking advantage of the other but you find it hard to put your finger on the problem. Try asking some questions to tease out what is happening. Is power being used to exert fair influence or to manipulate selfishly? What is the intended outcome? How aware are both parties of the situation? Are you both willing participants? What is the actual outcome? What degree of control is being exerted? By whom? Is one of you exploiting a position of trust or authority? Are mutual trust and respect being enhanced or destroyed? We are not usually in a position to judge all of these contributory factors, and, at the end of the day, probably our best way of knowing is to listen to our gut feeling.

ACCIDENTS

Some accidents are simply a route to time out. Recently I lost my footing on a cliff path and tumbled several yards down a steep hillside, coming to rest painfully against a large boulder. I suffered a cracked rib. What was remarkable was that I did not utter a sound from the time I lost my footing until after my friends helped me up. It was the thing they each remarked upon with amazement. To me it seemed quite 'natural'. Maybe it was because I was unconsciously trying to slip away unnoticed. The message from this fall was a reminder to retreat from company more often to allow time for reflection.

But falling may have many messages. People who have repeated accidents that involve minor damage, such as denting the car or breaking crockery may be suppressing anger. Clumsiness, losing personal items and forgetfulness, when they persist, often indicate preoccupation with other matters. A clumsy or forgetful woman may be stressed or reluctant to fully engage with the life she is leading, resenting the demands it makes on her. Similarly, appointments that are forgotten, rearranged or cancelled show someone who is indecisive, uncertain or lacking commitment. She may be spreading herself too thinly. These are all signs of someone who is not centred and grounded in her existence and who has found no other means of expressing this.

Donna Ladkin [11] describes a *"week of dislocation"* when her planned teaching seminar was not scheduled in students' timetables, her work was interrupted, trains were cancelled and delayed and she felt uncharacteristically powerless. Following these disruptions she stumbled down a flight of steps and came to the realisation *"I am not in my legs."* She recognises that at such times her centre of gravity is in her head or upper chest:

> "I feel easily knocked about by what is going on around me. I feel less able to make good decisions for myself. I often feel 'whoosy', 'phased'. I'm not good at taking cues of what is happening around me."

So if you are prone to accidents, forgetfulness or falling, ask yourself, why? Why did I need to be stopped in my tracks, to be forced to rest, to be grounded? What have I fallen *into*? Let the answer come from your body.

BODY SYMPTOMS AND ILLNESS

Unexpressed emotion has to find some outlet and will lodge in some part of the body, often lying dormant for years, but ultimately causing dis-ease in that part. Louise Hay [12], Gill Edwards [13] and Carolyn Myss [14] are among those writers and therapists who have explored the meaning of illness in depth. In their studies of dis-ease they associate particular psychic meanings to the different parts of the body affected by illness. Their case studies show that it is possible to find healing by linking symptoms to the original traumatic event and releasing the associated emotions. If you don't find their analysis helpful or can't 'see' its relevance to your situation, try simply asking the part of your body that is affected, as suggested in Chapter 7.

Making these links is not always clear and immediate. It may take a long time to decode or wake up to body messages. For Flora, a devoted wife and mother, the recognition came too late.

Flora was a gentle person with a wry sense of humour, who was always ready to listen to the problems of others and to lend a hand where it was needed. Flora's silence ultimately killed her. First came the suppressed anger at being pressured into marriage by her family when she became pregnant. Later, loyalty to her man kept her silent on the subject of his alcoholism for twenty years of marriage. Her unspoken anger found its expression through illness, in the form of a cancer that ate away at her internally. It finally erupted and quickly spread, just as she was looking forward to some freedom:

> *"Just as I was planning time for myself. I was going to learn Italian, it's something I've always wanted to do."*

Instead she shrunk away. Her husband refused to believe that she was going to die and so denied her the chance to voice her concerns about the future of their children. She was silenced to the last.

Many sensations and symptoms appear in our language when we use physical metaphors to describe emotions. For example: 'he's eaten up with resentment', 'she's a pain in the neck', 'that really get's up my nose', 'I've got you under my skin'. Take some time to consider whether your favourite expressions reflect the minor ailments that you tend to suffer from.

DRINKING

There are times when alcohol can help a woman to be more fully herself. It relaxes the tightness in the belly, throat and jaw and allows some of the true self to emerge. But it can also deaden the sense of self. On the one hand you may gain confidence, a temporary effervescence and the illusion of a glittering personality, but on the other, you pay the price of being out of touch with your true feelings.

Anita drank in the first place to conform:

> "My mother gave me my first drink when I was ten or eleven. It was some special occasion and she insisted I drank this sherry. It was disgusting, I didn't want it, but she said I had to learn to drink. It wasn't so much learning to handle alcohol. It was about bringing me up not to be boring like her family who were teetotallers. She said that people who didn't drink weren't any fun."

Mixing with a fast set in her teenage years ensured that Anita learned her lesson well. Years later she remembered it when she was finding it no fun at all struggling with two small boys at bedtime:

> "I'd get so uptight with them squabbling that I just wanted to knock their heads together. I'd yell as well and that made it much worse. Then I started having a drink while they were having their tea. It made all the difference. I was relaxed, playful. I got absorbed in their world and we had fun."

At this stage her drinking was a secret but later became a protest:

> "I was definitely saying something by drinking more than my husband thought I should. Partly it was like a rebellion. The more he checked the level in the bottle, the more I'd pour another glass. But I suppose it was also something like, 'I can no longer bear this marriage unless I drink'. It was something we couldn't talk about. It was the only way to say it. I couldn't face it at that stage."

Anita did not become an alcoholic. Years later she realised that her body could no longer process the amount of alcohol she was consuming. She was in a new relationship and this was a language she no longer needed to speak. Now she drinks for the pleasure of a good wine with a meal or to celebrate an occasion. Her whole system has responded to the change and she enjoys the extra energy she has when she doesn't drink.

Consider your own relationship with alcohol. It is important not to judge your answers. If a judging voice creeps in, ask whose it is, where it comes from. Whether you never drink alcohol or you have some every day, ask why? What does it meant to you? What are the positives and negatives it brings into your life? What are your feelings about reflecting in this way? Simply notice and move on.

More extreme forms of the language of silence include self-harming, eating disorders and suicidal cries for help. The sufferer's self-esteem has sunk so low, or has never been given the chance to grow.

EXERCISE – GOING INTO YOUR SILENCE

Allow yourself at least half an hour of uninterrupted time, more if possible. Make the usual preparations.

Consider each of the following questions:

How have you been affected by silence?

What are the secrets that you keep or the things you keep silent about?

What would be the consequences of being more open?

How might you move towards greater openness?

Who would you choose to talk to?

How might you prepare?

BECOMING VISIBLE

In spite of the Victorian maxim that children should be seen but not heard, it is my experience that silence and the tendency to feel invisible or to seek anonymity go hand in hand.

To succeed in public life women have to be prepared to become more visible. The strategy of keeping a low profile is no longer a viable option. Another aspect of moving into the public world is that we usually move out of a predominantly female world, into a predominantly masculine one. The transition from a female, 'kitchen' communication style, to a male, 'front of house' style involves a lot of presentation, both of the person and of that which is to be communicated. It is not only a question of language (not shared, so needing to be more explicit), but of packaging that signals a communication to be delivered. Often a woman's contribution is not seen or heard, and therefore ignored, because she fails to draw attention to it in a way that the masculine world will recognise. How often have you had your suggestion ignored in a meeting? How often have you heard that same suggestion greeted with enthusiasm when put forward by a man minutes later? As found by Mary Belenky [15] and her co-authors, *"Even among women who feel they have found their voice, problems with voice abound. Some women told us, in anger and frustration, how frequently they felt unheard and unheeded – both at home and at work."*

Often women do not even recognise the competence they have. For example, it is common for women returning to paid work after a period running the home and family to have a serious crisis of confidence. They may have been juggling the conflicting demands of a partner, children, parents and dog, feeding and clothing them all on a minimal allowance, running a laundry, gardening, cleaning and taxi service, to say nothing of helping with homework in the evening. And yet they feel incompetent. They do not readily translate these mundane activities into the highly transferable skills of time management, mediation, negotiation, motivation, diplomacy, budgeting, coaching, presentation and stress management skills.

Women easily fall into thinking that what we have to offer is trivial, homespun and belongs in the privacy of the kitchen, where we were safe and our contribution looked valid. When we emerge into that outside world we are vulnerable and exposed and it is painful to have other eyes 'trivialising' our 'homespun' offering. We long for that privacy to hide our shame and shut out the critical gaze.

What of this image of the kitchen? It suggests that out-of-the-way place where women have traditionally belonged in the eyes of many men, where the hard labour takes place. If a woman shares that view, her kitchen will feel like a domestic prison. But, if she takes charge of the situation, she can make it a place for the richness of women sharing. It can become the creative, focal heart of the household, company or community where women are at the centre.

And what of the eyes that we imagine look so scornfully upon our kitchen offerings? They may of course be scornful, on the basis that even if you are paranoid, it doesn't mean they aren't out to get you. Alternatively what we mistake for scorn may be wondering, awe, puzzlement, fear or longing. So it is vital that we contain our paranoia and entertain the possibility of communication to convey what we are about and have it understood.

Much of women's difficulty in this context comes from being brought up to be inconspicuous and not to attract attention. A warning phrase I remember from childhood as the ultimate deterrent was *"people will look at you"*. A fact we have to come to terms with in a more public life is that people will indeed look at us. Women have traditionally been taught to blend - with the wallpaper in the case of wallflowers, with the crowd, but most of all with the man. In many new situations we take on the chameleon role. We call it testing the temperature of the water, but actually it is being afraid to be ourselves until we are sure the new people are pussycats and not tigers. Often by then it is too late to change our behaviour. We have already been cast in a role or ignored. Or they are indeed tigers, and if we had only bounced in being positively ourselves and unafraid, they would have eaten out of our hands. As it is they will eat us for breakfast if we rattle the cage. You can't make a glorious entrance if you've been sitting in the room for some time.

I once attended a workshop where Leslie Kenton was facilitating part of the day. I shall never forget the presence she displayed in making her entrance. Although we were all standing round in small groups chatting when she came in, I doubt that many people missed it. It wasn't so much what she was wearing that caught the attention, eye-catching though that was, but the way she moved, with poise and panache. She was wearing a white shirt, a richly embroidered waistcoat, and a white skirt that swirled just above high-heeled red shoes. There was a red band in her long blonde hair and a red sash at her waist.

Part of me (in my puritan grandmother's voice) said, "show-off!" Another part admitted jealousy, and another frankly admired what I saw: a woman who was not afraid to step fully into her power and own it. This last impression was confirmed when she kicked off the red shoes and started to work with us as a group. This was no show-off. This was someone who worked respectfully with everyone present, knew what she was doing and was doing it supremely well.

Being visible is directly the opposite of being a chameleon. Obviously! Visibility involves having the courage of our convictions and speaking up for them. Once we've been visible we have to keep it up. It is not possible to slip into oblivion again because people have expectations of us and we develop an obligation to do the best for those people. But most of all we owe it to ourselves, to our soul selves, to live to our potential.

EXERCISE – YOUR JOB DESCRIPTION

This exercise is particularly appropriate for women who are not in paid work.

Put some time aside – at least half an hour. Make the usual preparations.

Draw 3 columns on a piece of paper.

In the first column, list all the domestic tasks you undertake in a typical day or week.

In the second column, against each task write the name of the skill that is required to succeed in this task.

In the third column, write the term that would be used to describe this skill in a work setting.

For example: sorting out two small boys who are squabbling over toys requires you to be assertive, firm and patient, to listen, and to get them to negotiate. These are all skills required of a mediator who resolves conflict situations in the workplace.

MIRRORING

A mirror is a useful transitional tool for anyone wanting to become visible. Have you ever looked at yourself in a mirror and experienced surprise at seeing a competent adult looking back at you when you have been feeling childish and insecure inside? A mirror, whether made of glass or metaphor, is an important piece of equipment as we search for credibility in the transition from the kitchen to the front of house.

We constantly need to check the changes of image and presentation that we make. *Has it slipped? Is it really OK? Does it still look right? Is it really me?* These are some of the questions for which we seek answers and reassurance.

Even as babies we use the mother's face as a mirror to develop our sense of identity. When it reflects back love and consistency it feeds our self-esteem and confidence. Similarly, as adults we use other people's responses to develop our adult identity as it grows and changes.

There is a distinction to be made between self-esteem and self-confidence. Self-esteem involves feeling good *internally* and loving oneself. Self-confidence, on the other hand, consists of acting effectively *externally*, particularly in high profile situations. Being high in one and low in another leads to traits which may appear inconsistent to outsiders.

For instance, people who are high on self-confidence (like actors and celebrities) may surprise us when they reveal a sense of inadequacy or depression based on low self-esteem behind the public persona. They may be fine performers on stage with a big audience, but shy and hesitant when meeting informally with one or two people. On the other hand, people with sound self-esteem and low self-confidence, who have worked at becoming more assertive, often fail to recognise their own progress and need to bring their own picture of themselves more in line with the perception of others.

Sally was a clerical officer who had started work as a filing clerk. Hearing how other people saw her on a training and development course allowed her to compare the image that they had of her with the image that she had of herself. She reflected:

> "It gave me the idea that whilst you **know** yourself better than other people know you, the way they **see** you may be more accurate than the way you see yourself. I realised that I needed to update my self-image."

Looking back, she knew that she had coped well with some particularly difficult circumstances and had managed to take control when necessary. But she still felt insecure and lacked confidence. It was only when she looked at these contradictory messages that she realised that she was really much stronger and more capable than she had previously believed. She always could cope, but often didn't *feel* that she could. Now she became convinced. With this new insight and conviction Sally's career took off. She was quickly promoted, decided to study for qualifications and was soon in a position to choose a new direction for herself.

Sally made a distinction between her internal, private self and the self that she made available to others. She began to see that her confident *"out there"* self could nurture her inner self:

> *"For a long time I was only using my strength and energy in crises, generally to support others. Now I also use the same energy for my own benefit."*

Sally points the way here to developing a healthier relationship with self, which has a message for all of us about finding ways of building our energy and using it, not only to benefit others but also to nurture ourselves. In this way we create a positive spiral rather than the vicious circle of depletion and exhaustion we so often experience.

Stop and consider whether your own self-image needs an update. Look back over a few years and notice what you have achieved or come through in that time. Are you the same person? Ask some trusted friends how you come across to them or how you have changed. Look in the mirror and say to yourself 'I am a strong/wise/confident woman.' Find the right words for you – challenging but accurate. And remember, in the words of Marianne Williamson [16], *"Your playing small doesn't serve the world."* Remember to use your growing strength to nurture your inner child.

THE SOUND OF SILENCE BREAKING

In many situations as a facilitator I was privileged to listen to the *"sound of silence breaking"*,[1] and to appreciate at first hand how *"the development of a sense of voice, mind, and self were inextricably intertwined"*.[17] Programmes that develop assertiveness are often the setting for a woman to break out of a long habit of passivity and silence. In seeking a fitting expression of her repressed emotion she will tend to roar, swinging into extremes of aggression. So much has been dammed up for so long. It may have seeped out in unsatisfactory tears or it may have had no outlet. Now there is no stopping the eruption or the seemingly endless need to talk. It will be some time before such a woman will be ready to calm herself into the middle way of assertive behaviour, or to be the patient listener she once was. The stories here are of some women who decided it was time to break out of invisibility and silence into making their mark on the world.

Some women, like Sophie, who may be confident and articulate at work may revert to comparative silence at home. Sophie used her secretarial job as a stepping stone. When we met her before, she described how she'd been *"a good little girl"* as a child and how the secretarial role was in a similar mould. She had noticed how managers *"nearly fall over when a secretary takes the initiative and makes an intelligent contribution."* However, Sophie did well in her job and rose to executive secretary where she confidently advised directors on people management issues:

> *"But at home I was like a mouse. I'd do anything my husband wanted. I never protested when he bossed me around. He expected me to be like his mother always was, picking up after him while he never lifted a finger. The people at work would never have believed it if they could have seen me at home. I suppose I was quite a split personality."*

Sophie's job, and the development courses she attended, helped her to grow up. She felt as if she was waking from a deep sleep. When her husband refused to consider change she left the relationship and shortly afterwards made her career change.

Several images stay with me of women who broke their silence on Returning to Work courses. Whether middle or working class, native English speakers, or learning the language having recently arrived in this country, they all identified becoming articulate as an important goal on the way to realising their independence, assertiveness, or self-fulfilment. Some women may have lost this ability through being immersed in domesticity, talking mainly with children and conversing with other adults at a practical rather than a conceptual level. Others may or may not have had these problems, but are contending with the learning of a new language and culture. What all of these women are also doing is naming themselves, and finding their own identity.

It may be, like Lyn, that they were never articulate, came out of school with the label "thick", and received nothing but destructive criticism at home. Lyn tended to look quickly behind her when she spoke, as if the sound might be coming from someone else. She came across to the group and to me as a strong, witty woman, but could not imagine herself being employable because she was *"no good at nuffin."* She told us that she always parked near the entrance of a car park in order to avoid the self-conscious ordeal of having to walk across it. She was frightened to go out without her children because she felt *"unreal"* and invisible on her own.

Lyn started to identify her goal by wishing that she could *"talk posh"*. Discussion in the group brought her to the conclusion that, although she still wished that, it was more important to be able to express what was in her head and talk about things for which she currently had no words.

The vast majority of these women were driven by the search for their own potential. They had considered their domestic existence and said a firm 'no' to the question *"is this all there is?"* and were seeking their own development in whatever form it might take. Often they had made a specific decision to avoid returning to previous occupations, even when they had the skills and qualifications to make this the easier option

Julie had very recently 'come out', in the sense of returning to the world after conquering agoraphobia and a fear of meeting new people. She had a terror that her 'problem' made her unacceptable. When she became nervous, which she was most of the time, her head nodded in a way she could not control. Her excitement at her new self won through however, and having broken her silence, she talked eloquently of her experience. She was also a good listener and able to support others in their struggle. While on the course Julie secured a job interview for which she practised with the help of other women. I later heard that she succeeded in getting the job, her first in about fifteen years.

Leila was a courageous Muslim woman who went on to attend an Access course for people returning to higher education. When I first met her she spoke inaudibly with averted eyes, her head swathed in a heavy silk veil. Her struggle was a hard one, involving antagonising her mother-in-law and the risk of losing her husband as the price of breaking her silence and becoming visible. When she left the course, her head was held high and free of the veil, she looked people in the eye and spoke gently but clearly. She secured a University place to study Law and it was to the credit of both her and her husband that he supported her in this.

Stephanie was a Jewish woman who was well dressed, groomed and manicured, and spoke of a very affluent lifestyle. Stephanie broke silence in a different kind of way. She talked too much from the first, stole 'air time' from others, and was unable to maintain eye contact. Her talk concealed an underlying silence: she had not been communicating with herself, or allowing herself to acknowledge her own deep distress. She preferred to focus on externals, particularly being judgmental of others. She was cynical at first about the usefulness of the course in general, and was critical and scornful of both the content and the other people in the group. At the same time she could not help being curious about therapies of all sorts. As time went on she started contradicting her own strongly voiced opinions, and became more reflective. Finally she became more open about her emotions. She told us of conflicts in her life that she herself had not wanted to face before, let alone admit to others. Stephanie demonstrated that silence can be eloquent, and chatter a form of silence.

CREATIVE SILENCE

"A wise woman turns within for answers,
Knowing there's a place deep inside,
Holding her truth.
She becomes quiet enough to let the clarity of
Her inner voice shimmer through.
And then she listens." [18]

In the kind of silence referred to as 'mountain behaviour', we can each listen to our inner voice and tap into an age-old source of healing. We can grow this creative silence at the centre of our being and learn to expand it. The stillness and silence of mountains impressed me deeply during a holiday in Northern Spain. The phrase that kept coming to me was that the mountains were 'holding the silence'. To witness that, and to be held within that all-encompassing stillness was a profoundly restorative experience. It made me realise how little most of us experience deep silence and how much we need it.

In creative silence we can stretch out mentally, emotionally and spiritually as on calm water. It is a still pool rather than a stagnant pond. We can float on it and dip in and out of it as we wish. If we share this silence with others, then we are fully open to each other, in communication. This silence is open to interruption but it cannot be broken.

In such a silence we can reach inside and connect with our real spontaneous self. In doing so we also connect with the sacred.

Christina Baldwin [19] describes *"this point of silence ... the center of the self"*, while John Fox [20] echoes the dual nature of this kind of silence as a stillness *"where you meet with the essence of things"* and *"a place where we can go to meet ourselves."*

Clarissa Pinkola Estés writes about this meeting with ourselves in terms of the wild woman archetype, and the very particular alchemy of La Loba, the Wolf Woman. La Loba collects the bones of wolves until she has a complete skeleton. She then sings it into life, and the wolf transforms into a wild, free, woman.

> *"... when she has assembled an entire skeleton, when ... the beautiful white sculpture of the creature is laid out before her ...*
>
> *"... she sings out ... the wolf creature begins to breathe. ... La Loba sings so deeply that the floor of the desert shakes and ... the wolf ... runs away down the canyon."* [21]

We engage in a similar kind of alchemy by using our silence well. We can use the stillness simply to empty and refresh our minds. Or we can use it to take stock of our day, our week, our life and where we are going. We can use it to write poetry or draw or paint. We can keep a journal and do all of those things within its pages. However we choose to use it, our awareness and intention will bring our real selves to life in a silence that is rich and fertile, and which may give birth to a song.

EXERCISE – CLAIMING SOLITUDE

Put some time aside – at least half an hour. Make the usual preparations.

Savour the experience you have just gained for yourself away from the busy-ness of your day and the demands of others.

> Empty your mind of pre-occupations. When they drift in, just notice and wave them goodbye again.
>
> Let peaceful images fill your mind.
>
> Commit to yourself to make regular time for private and reflective silence in your day
>
> When could you find this time?
>
> For how long? Half an hour or more is good, but ten or even five minutes is better that nothing.
>
> How can you ensure that you are not disturbed?
>
> Where? How will you set the scene for a peaceful environment?
>
> Write down your plans to achieve this necessary nourishment for yourself.

What would your Wise Woman do?

She would slow down and breath, listening to the silence.

Then she would know what to say.

214 - THE WISE WOMAN WITHIN

– CHAPTER 12 –

MAKING A SONG AND DANCE

*"I danced in the morning when the world was begun,
I danced in the Moon and the stars and the Sun,
I was called from the darkness by the song of the Earth,
I joined in the singing and She gave me birth."*

Folksong[1]

So how have we progressed in this exploration of women's ways of knowing? What is the benefit of being better acquainted with the wise woman we carry within us? Who is she? Has she given you a glimpse of the goddess? What is her wisdom? You might like to examine your position by gently asking yourself some of the following questions: Are you more comfortable with yourself as a result? Are you healthier? More mentally alert? Able to express, control and manage your emotions? Have you found ways to be peaceful? What does your awareness of connection with the natural world bring into your life? How does inhabiting your body more fully affect your ability to relax, have fun, laugh and cry? Are you finding a more even balance between being a mountain and being a teapot?

The chances are that you will not have answered a definitive 'yes' to many of the questions above. For it is not a matter of meeting the wise woman within and having an instant make-over. Getting to know her is a process that happens gradually and organically over time. You will probably meet her and forget her name a number of times, just as happens with people in social situations. Then both the encounters, and the pattern of how and when they occur, will become more significant. She will become your friend, and although you may neglect her from time to time, her friendship will become so valuable that eventually she will be a constant companion.

The ways in which you have been getting to know your wise woman have probably been largely solitary, private and quiet, involving reflecting, visualising, writing, drawing and walking. It's time to get moving, to make a noise and seek the company of other women. A discussion group is a good starting point. It enables women to share their experience and discover that they are not alone. If it is safely and sensitively facilitated, such a group can offer invaluable support. But for a true connection to the wise woman I have come to realise that we need to get away from words and talk, however powerfully such talking engages our emotions. We need to get out of our heads and back to our physical roots. We need to practise the more primitive activities that women have traditionally shared. We need to dance and sing. I do not mean the kind of dancing that involves learning steps or singing that follows a musical score. I mean movement that lets the body feel its connection to the earth and the natural sound that pours from an open throat. In this kind of moving and toning it is impossible to be out of step or out of tune in the conventional sense. Once we lose our almost inevitable self-consciousness, these activities join us together, strengthening our links with the ancestors and allowing our body pulse to resonate with the rhythms of the natural world.

This is the most fundamental kind of communication. It pre-dated language when, as Wendy Buonaventura[2] comments, *"the main vehicle of self-expression was the body"*. Paul Newham[3] describes early communication as *"an acoustic gesture, a voice-dance"*, noting how the whole body and voice was involved together, assuming *"a thousand different shapes"* to re-enact a single event. As language developed it was capable of expressing abstract thought, but there remain some things that only the body can express.

Nina, whose dancing was described earlier, found her way back to re-inhabit her body through movement. The experience of childhood abuse meant that she had left her body as a way of protecting herself. Her dancing started as a communication with her body, tentative at first, but growing in delight at the response of her whole system, a mutual recognition where self and body became one in exorcising the past and celebrating the union. Nina's ritual dancing to her group of supportive women was a true example of self-expression, *"a showing rather than a showing off"*, as Buonaventura describes women's dance.[4] What Nina was showing us was her potential for wholeness, the beginning of a long process of healing during which she was to come more and more to her real self.

Most of us refer to the body as something that is distinct from the self. We talk to the body and about it as a separate entity. As somebody recently said to me, "it is not I". He recognised the contradiction in what he was saying, but was nevertheless caught in it. It can be argued that this separation of mind and body has freed the human spirit and intellect and made great achievements possible. We can however also appreciate that spiritual and intellectual power can be dangerous if it is not grounded in the earth and humanity. The separation of right brain from left brain, of body from mind, of feeling from thinking, of intuition from logical analysis has had far-reaching consequences for the planet, expressed by the pioneering psychologist and researcher, Jean Houston:

> *"Quite simply, the holocaust of body-mind has led to the ecological holocaust and to the awful inadequacy of present political and economic solutions."* [5]

Through her work, using movement and sound, Houston aims to begin to heal the body-mind split which she feels has led to *"real loss of human intelligence"* in the Western world.[5] Using ancient and modern methods from varied cultures, she develops exercises to awaken and stretch under-used faculties, *"to open the lenses and unshackle the minds"*. One of Houston's aims is to improve our 'multi-tracking' ability. This can shift us out of a one-track perception of reality into a more richly textured mental and emotional life. Do you remember as a child rubbing your tummy in a circular movement with one hand, while patting the top of your head with the other? It's the same principle.

Some exercises involve a constant barrage of mental and physical surprises combined with vigorous movement, sound and the need for acute concentration. I shall never forget the experience of being talked through one of these exercises in a group. As I remember, I was swinging my arms from side to side, running on the spot and singing Rule Britannia, while thinking about the Eiffel Tower, a traffic jam on the M25 and a hive of bees. If you want to experiment with the exercises in Jean Houston's book, record them onto a tape or have someone read them aloud, making changes to the images and songs appropriate to your cultural background.

Other exercises are quiet and reflective, involving inner dialogue and equally stretching imaginal gymnastics. All aim to extend us beyond the territory of the known into an altered state of consciousness that allows us to see the infinity of potential that Houston knows is available to us, but which we don't use.

EXERCISE – ON EXERCISE

Put some time aside – at least an hour. Make the usual preparations.

Spend 10 minutes writing down all the ways in which you exert your body fully by stretching it rather than stressing it – that is, striding out on a walk without constraints, rather than clipping along on high heels with a brief case, or struggling with heavy shopping bags.

Consider the difference between hard physical work using your hands or low-tech tools and working with electrical gadgets or power tools. Don't get into "right answers" here. Just notice the difference.

> How many times in a day or a week do you work up a sweat or get out of breath? Does this happen often enough to tone your circulation and metabolism? Does it happen in the course of an activity that you enjoy? Plan how you could do this more often or take more pleasure in it.
>
> Now go out and take your body for a walk, listening carefully to what it really needs.

MOVEMENT AND BALANCE

At a very simple level we are aware that physical movement works upon the mind to stimulate or expand its creativity. You will know this already from the experience of problems that 'solve themselves' during a walk or a shower. In situations where fear causes us to freeze, we can learn to break the pattern by using movement. This was brought home to me repeatedly when teaching presentation skills to managers in industry. Nervousness made these young professionals wooden either in voice tone and modulation, or in physical posture and movement. Some would not move at all; others glued their eyes to the slide screen; others looked towards the audience, skating over their heads without making eye contact. Many used minimal gestures involving the head but not the shoulders, kept their elbows pinned at the waist, or held on to one arm as if afraid that it might escape. All these habits contributed to what I called the 'plastic personality', which was like a strait jacket that otherwise confident people put on when they walked centre stage to present. It was as if the eyes of the audience caught them like a rabbit frozen in the beam of the headlights.

Robin had all these characteristics. He was an otherwise competent professional who regularly dried up when speaking, because of nervousness. He was the first of many to receive the very simple advice to *"Come clean when you dry. Tell the audience that you have totally forgotten what you were going to say next."* Robin found that this had several advantages. By taking pressure off the brain, his memory recovered spontaneously, and if this didn't happen it gave him 'permission' to refer to his notes. It made him feel more 'real' and in control, and he also *looked* much more in control than when standing with flapping jaw and burning face. By keeping the audience informed, this strategy avoided antagonising listeners and even gained their support.

Presenters also worked at preventing the paralysis in the first place by using a physical warm-up and building movement into their presentations. By staying 'in the body' they were able to avoid falling victim to the 'plastic personality'.

Adrian spoke of controlling his anger at being disempowered by bureaucracy. He noticed that this led to a tendency to paralysis and produced a vicious circle. He too was focusing attention on staying present and found a metaphor while watching some rabbits:

> *"There were two rabbits in amongst the trees, bouncing around, chasing each other with little white tails going. There was ever such a lot of energy in that. And it just reminded me that the energy's out there. It's a happy kind of energy. There are two images – of them bouncing, full of fun with their ears up, and then they get the foot thump and they're away down the hole again."*

Adrian considered how it would be to give himself the instruction to *"stay out there"*. He recognised that his tendency to *"fall into a hole"* or become not-present in his body, was simply an old learned response to get back in the burrow and avoid getting hurt. It was possible to choose to take the risk of staying present and not shutting down the energy. This involved trusting that the connection with the energy and momentum he saw in the rabbits would carry him through any challenges.

> "... it requires doing the one thing that we seek to avoid at all costs: we are asked finally to put our entire bodies into a situation; to refuse numbness and protection in favour of risk and immediacy." [6]

We need the ability to laugh, and yet to hold gravity within that laughter; to be open and also be prepared to fence a little; to dance and hold our ground; to allow chaos while maintaining focus; to spin with a still centre.

Sadie experimented with this risk-taking on a Ropes Challenge course.[7] Working as a change consultant in a complex organisation, she repeatedly found herself thrown off balance in negotiation with senior managers. Sadie asked the questions:

"Why do I always need to be balanced? What would it be like to be out of balance? Can I be out of balance and still be OK? I set out to play with being physically out of balance as a metaphor for my work experience. The climax of the experiment involved jumping from a telegraph pole. I found that letting go was the challenge, but the fall itself was fun. Falling was fun as love has been! I did something completely out of character before I jumped. I drew attention to myself! I saw a friend way down the field and I yelled for him to watch me. I found it a relief to be letting go of a sense of who I am, letting go of things that were previously fixed and important and feeling relief at not having to get it right or follow the rules."

Sadie experienced a moment of trusting her instincts and her body, just as she had when falling in love, without holding back to calculate the consequences. It was a moment of coming to herself. It is significant that she also deliberately chose to be spontaneous in earlier group activities. She took an active role, took the lead and contributed ideas in an uncharacteristic way, that is, without editing or censoring her behaviour. Sadie's final comment on the course is telling. She notices that, in situations of uncertainty, she too readily moves to support others, rather than examining what she needs to do for herself. *"Then I get lost in that support role,"* she comments.

Maybe she is at a stage in her organisational work where she might take less time considering the likely impact of her interventions. Rather she might focus on expressing her views clearly and unequivocally, without wrapping them up in concern for others, which may convey a confusing double message. Or she might simply concentrate on enjoying the dance in meeting unexpected challenges.

EXERCISE – LOSING BALANCE

You might like to experiment with your own "Dance of Difference" by taking yourself off balance in small ways. Later you can try some bolder activities like Sadie's if it suits you.

Simply try interrupting your normal patterns and behaving differently. Try voicing an opinion where you would normally be quiet, or choose to be silent in a meeting where you would usually take a lead.

Abandon routines for a day, eat different food, wear a new colour or dress in beautiful clothes just for your own pleasure.

Keep the TV and radio switched off for a day and see how it is to hear no news and listen to your own thoughts. Or, if your house is normally quiet, play music and see how it affects you.

DANCE OF LIFE

I found it delightful to discover that the English word 'dance' comes from the Sanskrit *'tanha'* meaning 'joy of life', while the Arabic and Turkish words derive their meaning from celebration.[8] For dance does express joy and dancing seems to generate rather than expend energy.

"By its very nature it [dance] is one of the most powerful means of auto-intoxication we have, developing energy in the body and then releasing it." [9]

Dance used to be an integral part of religious ritual when natural cycles were seen as mysterious forces and spirits were thought to inhabit every part of the natural world. This is still the case in some remote cultures, and the belief systems live on in shamanic work the world over. A shaman uses movement and sound, in the form of drumming, rattling or chanting, as a tool to help him or herself to fully inhabit the body and to induce the state of consciousness that makes a shamanic journey possible. Similarly, in the old religion, the release of energy in a trance dance produced an altered state of consciousness, which helped the dancer to unite with the deity and absorb the power of the goddess. Fertility, sexuality and spirituality went hand in hand in a religion that centred around the magical creative powers of women and where priestesses conducted rituals. This fusion of body and spirit is a far cry from the principles of the male-dominated religions that ousted the old beliefs. As both Christianity and Islam sought to destroy the rituals of goddess worship, women became feared and mistrusted.[9] Religious practices moved away from the cycles of the seasons and human fertility towards a more driven and masculine pattern, which no longer reflected the ebb and flow of natural energy.

Matthew Fox identifies this new pattern in the spiritual practices described in the Old Testament. He sees the ladder in Jacob's dream as a symbol of a spiritual path that takes us up to God and away from the earth and the grounded feminine principle:

"Perfection is upward. There can be no question that this drive upwards in the name of spirituality is a drive away from body, earth, matter, mother, the sensual." [10]

This has resulted in western worship becoming *'worshup'*. Fox suggests that, instead of *"climbing Jacob's ladder,"* we learn to *"dance

Sarah's circle" to invoke a more life-enhancing principle. For the story of Sarah conceiving a child focuses on human emotions of joy and surprise. Sarah is a *"symbol of laughter and creativity"*. Fox comments that *"there is little laughter and joy among those who climb ladders. Ladder-climbing is ever so serious. Ego's are so much involved."* [10]

Jill Purce is another writer and spiritual worker who urges us to reconnect with natural rhythms through dance and sound. In her book, *The Mystic Spiral*, she describes the dance of the mystic Sufi Dervishes in which the dancer connects to the energy and vibration of the universe:

> *"He spins gradually faster, as if by his own revolutions he were connecting Heaven and earth by actually turning the spirit through himself and down into the ground, while his axis and heart remain absolutely still and his own spirit soars to its Divine Source."* [11]

Although our culture has forgotten the depths of meaning behind the dance, we may yet be open to activating that energy *"every time we 'turn' or circle, in the movement for example of Scottish dancing."* [11] A reminder of the fundamental meaning of dance comes unexpectedly from the scientific world. Fritjof Capra, writing in 1983, noted that physicists were using phrases such as *"dance of creation"* and *"energy dance"* when describing matter:

> *"Modern physics has shown us that movement and rhythm are essential properties of matter; that all matter, whether here on Earth or in outer space, is involved in a continual cosmic dance."* [12]

Each one of us is part of this spiralling dance of life. Every exploration we make brings us back to the centre, to the roots of our identity as women. We find the functions of our bodies in tune with the cycles of nature; in coming to terms with our personal history we can trace the patterns of generations coming full circle and moving beyond us; in understanding and expressing our griefs, fears and joys we learn to accept the troughs and peaks of our moods as part of a fertile process. We grow wiser and richer by aligning ourselves more closely with the cycles of the year, of night and day, of rest and activity.

We can step out of the victim mode of ever-decreasing circles, into the empowerment of the expanding spiral, keeping the thread of energy unbroken as it chains inward into the self and outward into the world. We can spin past the old paralysis, through the gaps between the words, through the crack between the worlds, into a still centre of knowing.

When we say we are centred, it means that we stand with awareness at the centre of all these cycles. It also means that the centre is within us and we are within the centre. We move in and out of the circle: now resting in the calm centre of the spiral, now spinning to the edge in an endless dance.

SOUND AND SINGING

The work of Jill Purce brings dance and sound together. She also teaches ancient voice techniques for healing and meditation:

"My aim is not modest, I am trying to re-enchant the world, which means to make it magical through chanting." [13]

Purce shares with Paul Newham a deep sense of "dis-enchantment" in the West where the culture of communal singing has largely been lost:

"... the conditioning we receive from parents and teachers who tell us we cannot sing, the sense of inadequacy instilled in those who do not read music and the overbearing preoccupations of everyday life — all these have led to a silencing of the true voice which in fact everyone possesses." [14]

As one of the many who had been told from childhood that I could not sing, I enrolled on one of Frankie Armstrong's Voice Workshops when I was forty. I was relieved to find that she did not ask us to sing. In fact she never referred to singing, but taught me the first steps to reclaiming my voice. First she asked us to examine our relationship with our voice, and went on to introduce rhythmic physical exercises that simulated the work of peasants in the fields. In no time she had the group chanting in time with their 'work'. The movement helped to release the sound, the sound encouraged the movement and we were soon too engaged in the rhythm and the energy of the activity to be self-conscious. As we grew tired, it quickly became clear to us how folk songs originally emerged as a necessary accompaniment to hard labour to keep up the momentum.

Sadie discovered this on the preparation day of her Ropes Challenge course. This day focused on building trust in the group, introducing small challenges and teaching basic safety procedures and support systems. Sadie confessed herself to be *"tired, cold, awkward and bitchy inside at the amount of detail-learning that was required at the end of an emotionally challenging day."* She only managed to cope with learning the procedures when she and two others developed a rhythmic dance and chant to memorise the sequence of actions involved.

This combination of physical movement and sound transforms our energy, especially when shared, as Sadie discovered. The voice is the bridge between mind and body, capable of a huge range of sophisticated modulations and intellectual fluency, as well as the guttural, non-verbal sounds of sensual expression. Our voice reflects the state of our physical and emotional health and our energy levels. When you telephone a close friend they will know immediately if you are upset or unwell by the tone of your voice. Even attempts to disguise your mood will fail, coming across as brittle to those who know you well. Paul Newham, the founder and director of the International Association for Voice Movement Therapy, recognises just how much *"our voices mirror the way we are."*[15] His work explores the potential for healing by releasing tensions through song and non-verbal sound. He uses systematic movement as an integral part of the process of releasing the voice, a "de-patterning" therapy which aims to reverse muscular habits relating to the voice. This retraining of the body is reminiscent of how the well-known Alexander Technique developed when Frederick Alexander, an actor, found himself losing his voice on stage. He noticed that his posture when he used his voice was constricting the airways and preventing his voice from escaping.

I have experienced this important link between movement and sound in workshop settings on several occasions. But a recent 'real life' example emphasised just how well it works. I had occasion to perform a vigorous dance for an important occasion and afterwards to attend a church service. Quite unexpectedly, when it came to singing the hymns, I found my voice soaring from an open throat. I am sure that I didn't always hit all the right notes, but I know that I was in tune with myself and I felt ecstatic.

Try to find a place where you can dance or sing or both. You may choose salsa or tap or belly dancing, ballroom dancing or Scottish reels, circle dancing or the dance of Gabrielle Roth's five rhythms.[16] Practitioners of the five rhythms are often to be found locally, and she has also produced a video called 'Ecstatic Dance'. There are so many different forms to choose from. If you can dance with a group of women, so much the better, but more importantly choose a group that is informal and a dance that your body finds irresistible.

Use every opportunity you have to loosen your voice – in the shower, in the car or while you do housework. But also look for chances to sing with others, whether in the pub, in church or in an informal group. If you need to build confidence in this area, there are many workshops advertised that aim to do just that.

EXERCISE – EARTH DANCE

Try this experiment at home.

Put some time aside – about half an hour. Find some rhythmic music that you like and play it at full volume when you have the house to yourself or the neighbours are out.

First take some time to stretch your limbs and shake them out as you breathe deeply to relax yourself and become present in your body.

Close your eyes, empty your mind and absorb the rhythm of the music. Start by standing limply, loosening your knees and letting your arms and head flop.

Gradually let your body respond as it wants to. You may want to stamp your bare feet into the ground, lift your arms in a slow circle or vibrate your legs from the knees so that your whole body shakes. The movement may be vigorous or gentle, minimal or bold, staccato or flowing.

Keep breathing as you move and open your mouth, letting any sound escape that wants to. Droning, humming, moaning or grunting, anything goes. As the momentum of movement increases, turn up the volume of sound you are making and free your voice to accompany your dance from an open throat.

Keep this up for a good 15 minutes or more. You will probably need to push yourself over the threshold of feeling silly and self-conscious into the open space where your dance and your voice and the music blend into one.

Give yourself time to wind down, physically and mentally, before emerging to rejoin others or resume everyday activities.

THE SACRED AND THE SPIRITUAL

When I started the process of writing, I did not intend this to be a book about spirituality. It was at first a question of avoidance, and later of not wanting to set the sacred and the spiritual apart from everyday activities. However, this dimension quickly became important and each chapter led in this direction. It seems a natural progression if we dig deeply enough into almost any aspect of life, and is most particularly true when exploring a matter of identity, our very nature as women. As we spin together the threads of our connection to the forces of the earth, our deep body knowing, our understanding of the past and the wisdom of the ancestors, we get glimpses of the bigger picture. We begin to sense our wholeness and our place in the scheme of the universe. The paradox is that this knowing is both complex and simple, mysterious and ordinary. It emerges from the centre of our being and belongs at the heart of the routines of our daily lives, whilst also connecting us to the stars.

Some of you may have experienced the exploration of the wise woman within as a search for the lost goddess of the golden age described in Chapter 1. In a sense we have been reawakening our ability to see the sacred in everything, at the heart of life, in everything we touch or undertake. We see the Maiden when we look back to our Child self, the Mother when we explore our adult achievements and the Crone when we look to the menopausal years. When we see the goddess manifesting as these stages in our own lives, it is easier to see that the sacred is to be found within us, just as it permeates the world around us. We just need that shift of perspective to see past the surface appearance of things, through the looking glass, into the crack between the worlds. Some of you may have had an 'Aha' moment of seeing in a different dimension, others may have had a series of glimpses or inklings which build over time.

Before we come to the end of this journey together, it would seem appropriate to clarify what we do and do not mean by spirituality and the sacred. Although spirituality and religion may be synonymous for some people, I make a clear distinction between the two. Confusing these led to me closing the door on spirituality for many years. I had been confirmed in the Church of England, but my commitment was short-lived. After the flurry of small cards depicting white doves and gentle Jesus had settled, and I had got over the disappointment that my new prayer book had a blue instead of a white cover, I began to notice that religion didn't feel right. It seemed to be more about elitism, guilt and damnation than anything positive.

As an adolescent, immersed in existentialism, it began to seem obvious to me that man created God in his own image rather than the other way round. I have a memory of myself hiding from the bible reading group, looking out at the stars and making some sort of pact with myself to go it alone without God.

Even after I realised that spirituality can exist without religious dogma, my attitude was one of tentative approach and suspicious avoidance. Spiritual growth turned out to be threatening, irrelevant, puzzling, funny and exciting.

So what do we mean by spirituality? For me, having a spiritual life means tuning in to a dimension beyond what we can perceive with our five senses. Some people find it easier to do this in nature, others in a church or temple, others when listening to music. It is possible to use a number of tools to help the process of tuning in to the spiritual dimension, such as ritual, candles, meditation, visualisation, tarot readings and the study of dreams. Sharing such rituals with other like-minded people also assists the process. In such a group drumming, dancing or chanting may be used to enter an altered state of consciousness which enhances the experience.

Honouring the sacred also means finding the extraordinary in ordinary activities and bringing joy and love into routines and everyday encounters. I don't mean pretending that we love everyone, but rather putting energy into seeing people as they really are. Nor do I mean cultivating the forced optimism that denies feelings of depression, boredom, pain, anxiety or frustration. We only find the joy if we fully accept our hurts and do something about them, wherever they come from.

When we attend regularly to spiritual practices we begin to see a glimpse of a pattern in our lives and a sense of being loved, guided and protected by a power beyond ourselves. There will be other times when we feel disconnected and cynical and the practices themselves seem ludicrous and empty. Alternatively you may simply not be ready to enter that realm at this time. Just because the mountain is there, it doesn't mean that you have to climb it.

The evidence for a spiritual dimension is overwhelming. The sense of the sacred seems to be shared across centuries and across all nations and cultures. When people travel to the boundaries of human experience they often come back with news of Spirit. The astronauts aboard Apollo 8, the first manned mission to go round the moon in 1968, responded with overwhelming awe and a reading from Genesis about the creation story. North American Indians send young men into the wilderness on a solitary quest to find their spirit guide as part of their initiation into manhood. Spending time in the spiritual dimension heightens our awareness of ourselves as an integral part of the cosmos. It expands our consciousness and our potential for wholeness, which is healing both for ourselves and for the planet.

MEETING WITH OTHER WOMEN

The process of becoming acquainted with the Wise Woman Within is much helped by joining with other like-minded women. Each woman's presence seems to act as a catalyst for others to share experience, contained and supported by the synergy of the group. Don't force the issue in finding such a group. You will find what you need when you need it, often in the most unexpected way.

Women have shared activities in circles since men first went hunting and they gathered to prepare food and make pots and clothes, forming a circle to contain the small children. Sharing an activity while sitting in a circle honours a natural rhythm of stillness and movement. It may be a circle where women meet to perform ritual. Or it may be a sewing circle, writing circle or a dance circle. Whether participants are aware or not, the dynamic of the circle is present. At the centre is a focus of stillness and the attention of members will rest there from time to time. The activity takes place at the edge of the circle, whether it be personal sharing, dancing, story-telling, sewing or gossip. Energy will pass around the edge of the circle in physical contact: scissors, conversation, glances, biscuits, laughter and tears. Everyone can see everyone else in a circle and everyone occupies a place of equal status. There is no head of a circle. To symbolise the energy of the circle place a candle or some flowers in the centre. It is pleasant to look at and gives a focus for reflection.

Whatever the activity, women benefit from gathering and being women together. Clarissa Pinkola Estés describes what we know so well:

> *"Women's ritual of being together, ... of belly talk, women talking from the guts, telling the truth, laughing themselves silly, feeling enlivened, going home again, everything better."* [17]

Friendships between women are special. They help us to know who we are and keep a sense of proportion. They are healing and nurturing. They soothe us when we are troubled and often fill the emotional gaps in relationships with partners. There is even a scientific basis for this belief, which I recently discovered. Scientists now suspect that hanging out with friends can counteract the stress that many of us experience on a daily basis. This news emerged from a study of stress reactions published in Psychological Review.[18] The study discovered that women respond to stress differently from men.

For decades, psychological research focused on the 'fight or flight' reaction to stress. This maintains that when confronted with stress, individuals either react with verbal or physical aggression, or withdraw from the stressful situation. It was thought that this applied equally to women and men. The new study found that 'fight or flight' holds good for men. But for women, this response doesn't make sense from an evolutionary standpoint. What female of any species would leave her baby to fend for itself while she physically takes on an aggressor? A female's first instinct would be to protect her children. In order to achieve that, she would bond with other females to create a mutually protective community.

Sure enough researchers found that women respond to stress with a cascade of brain chemicals that cause us to make and maintain friendships with other women. According to Dr. Klein of Pennsylvania State University, when the hormone oxytocin is released as part of the stress response in a woman, it buffers the fight or flight response and encourages her to tend children and gather with other women instead. When she actually engages in this tending or befriending, studies suggest that more oxytocin is released, which further counters stress and produces a calming effect. This calming response does not occur in men because the testosterone which men produce under stress seems to reduce the effects of oxytocin. Oestrogen, on the other hand, seems to enhance it.

You may like to consider whether you notice this 'tend-and-befriend' pattern in yourself and your women friends, in contrast to the 'fight-or-flight' behaviour pattern that we might expect to find as the principal method for coping with stress in men.

MAKING A SONG AND DANCE

In conclusion, however, I would like to focus on joy and celebration rather than stress. It is often the case that we do not make enough of the things in life we have to be thankful for. I do not want to hit a pious note of counting blessings here, but I do want to encourage you not to miss out on the opportunities for being happy. I know how easy it is to do. At one stage in my life I noticed that I was living with the person I loved, in a beautiful place and that all was well with my extended family. So how come I was feeling depressed rather than ecstatic? Noticing was the most important thing and enabled me to do some work to put this right. Part of that work was simply noting and articulating my good luck on a daily basis, and another, more difficult, part involved learning to accept that I deserved it. Because women are so good at adapting and 'making do', we are capable of making a habit of being less than happy. It's a way of being that is further encouraged by that laid-back part of our culture that undermines celebration and says it's 'uncool' to get too excited. This habit can drift back like a veil over real happiness if we do not make a conscious effort to throw it off. Maybe we need to learn and practise how to express joy and delight as freely as we express irritation and worry. Are we afraid that we don't deserve good fortune? Or that, if we draw attention to our blessings, they will be taken away? It seems far more likely that, if we don't appreciate them, they will fade away from neglect.

"Why do we have to make such a song and dance?" my father used to say. He came from a puritanical family where song and dance were certainly frowned upon. But what he was referring to was the time spent attending to details, usually associated with some kind of celebration, and usually overseen by my mother. It might be the presentation of food, the laying of a table, the wrapping of a present with coloured ribbons or the careful co-ordination of arrangements.

For years I was also impatient of this 'making a fuss' behaviour. I have since learned how such details can convey the caring that went into them, and what delight they can produce in both the giver and the receiver. They affect the quality of a welcome, demonstrate the love that comes with a gift, however small, and make friends feel as special as they are. It's all part of taking fun and celebration seriously, of putting energy into enjoyment.

Commit to yourself today to put energy into being a woman. Make a song and dance, both literally and metaphorically, to celebrate your qualities of womanliness. Go out and glory in the sights and cycles of nature and your connection with natural rhythms. Revel in your body and its sensuality. Wallow in an aromatic bath, savour delicious foods and wear rich colours and sensuous fabrics. Breathe deeply and stretch your limbs. Walk outside and appreciate the elements, whether they are cold and wet, warming or exhilarating. Find a time and a place where you can walk in the dark under the stars and bathe in the moonlight. Start a journal of your emotional and spiritual life. Take seriously the ghosts and traumas that you can't lay to rest by yourself and seek out a counsellor or therapist who can help you. Pay attention to your dreams and notice the pattern of your menstrual cycle if you have one. Befriend and nurture the Child in you, accepting and protecting her vulnerability and encouraging her playfulness and spontaneity. Listen to your mother, grandmother and aunts and explore the stories of your childhood and the history of the women of the family. See how it changes your understanding of them and your perspective on your own life. Take that experiment a stage further and visualise or fantasise about your more distant ancestors, until you have a sense of standing at the end of a long line of women whose support and experience you can draw on. Imagine that energy stretching beyond you into the future through the generations to come.

Above all, enjoy being a woman in all its richness and complexity, make a close companion of your Wise Woman Within and let her work her magic in the world.

What does your Wise Woman do?

She slows right down to find rhythm and balance,

She reaches out, and holds her own centre,

She knows how to play, and act with intent.

She treats her emotions like beautiful fireworks,

She takes herself seriously and laughs at herself,

She honours the past, and lives in the moment,

She values what is, is alert to potential.

She loves and respects the body she has,

And attends to the needs of its cycles.

She grows strong in her knowing that Earth is her mother,

She rests in the silence and finds her true voice.

When in trouble she talks to her women friends,

And listens and talks until the tears come,

She goes right on crying until she can laugh.

And then she knows what to do.

REFERENCES

Thanks and acknowledgement are given to all those people whose work I have referenced within these pages:

[1] Marianne Williamson, *Return to Love* (London: Thorsons 1992) pp.190-191. This quotation is Marianne Williamson's paraphrased interpretation of *A Course in Miracles*.

INTRODUCTION

[1] Cathy Cooper, *People Management*, 6th December 2001, p. 9; 23rd January 2003, p.11.

[2] Gemma Paris, "Get in touch with your feminine side" *People Management*, 21st March 2002, p. 25.

[3] Jon Watkins, "Spiritual Guidance" *People Management*, 20th February 2003, p. 16.

[4] Alan Briskin, "Significant Others" *People Management*, 21st March 2002, p. 50.

[5] Mary Field Belenky, Blythe McVicker Clinchy, Nancy Rule Goldberger and Jill Mattuck Tarule, *Women's Ways of Knowing: The Development of Self, Voice, and Mind* (New York: BasicBooks 1986) p. ix.

[6] Vicki Noble is a wise woman, writer, shaman and astrologer living in California.

[7] Vicki Noble & Karen Vogel, *Motherpeace Tarot cards*, 1981; Vicki Noble *Motherpeace: A Way to the Goddess through Myth, Art and Tarot* (New York: HarperCollins 1983).

[8] Merlin Stone, *When God was a Woman* (Orlando: Harcourt 1976).

CHAPTER 1 – BUILDING BRIDGES BETWEEN WORLDS

[1] Merlin Stone, *When God was a Woman* (Orlando: Harcourt 1976) p. 1.

[2] For a full account see Riane Eisler, *The Chalice and the Blade: Our History, Our Future* (London: Unwin Paperbacks 1990) particularly Chapters 2, 3 and 4.

[3] Barbara Walker, *The Women's Encyclopedia of Myths and Secrets* (New York: HarperCollins 1983) p. 187.

[4] To explore the symbolism read Anne Baring and Jules Cashford, *The Myth of the Goddess: Evolution of an Image* (London: Penguin Arkana 1993) Chapter 13.

[5] Jean Shinoda Bolen, *Crossing to Avalon* (New York: HarperCollins 1995) p. 80.

CHAPTER 2 – THROUGH THE EYES OF A CHILD

[1] R D Laing, *The Politics of Experience* (London: Penguin 1967) p. 60.

[2] Alice Miller, *The Drama of Being a Child* (London: Virago 1984) p. xi.

[3] Doris Lessing, *Memoirs of a Survivor* (London: Pan Books 1976) p. 10.

[4] Clarissa Pinkola Estés, *Women Who Run with the Wolves: Myths and Stories of the Wild Woman Archetype* (New York: Ballantine Books 1992) p. 15.

[5] Brian Patten, *The Minister for Exams* in *Armada* (London: Flamingo 1996).

CHAPTER 3 – EMOTIONAL HOUSEKEEPING

[1] Kahlil Gibran, *The Prophet* (London: William Heinemann 1980) p. 36.

[2] Gael Lindenfield, *Self Esteem* (London: Thorsons 1995) p. 22.

[3] Susan Jeffers, *Feel the Fear and Do it Anyway* (London: Century Hutchinson 1987).

[4] Gael Lindenfield, *Managing Anger* (London: Thorsons 1993).

[5] Daniel Goleman, *Working with Emotional Intelligence* (London: Bloomsbury 1999) p. 31.

[6] John Heron, *Feeling and Personhood* (London: Sage 1990) pp. 131-135.

[7] Denis Postle, *Emotional Competence*. Booklet. (London: Wentworth Institute 1992).

[8] Co-counselling works through self-help and mutual support. It aims to access potential which is locked away behind rigid and limiting behaviour patterns. The main method is to revisit past events and relive the emotions that were not fully expressed at the time. It is then possible to re-evaluate the past with the insight gained through this emotional purging process, and to use the energy released to live more fully. People are primarily taught *client skills* for doing emotional work. The *counsellor skills* mostly involve the ability to listen creatively and assist the client, who must always stay in charge of the session. For information about courses, visit the Co-counselling homepage at Sheffield University: www.shef.ac.uk/personal/c/cci/cciuk

CHAPTER 4 – DEVELOPING PERSONAL POWER

[1] Christiane Northrup, *Women's Bodies, Women's Wisdom* (London: Piatkus 1995) p. 479.

CHAPTER 5 – OUR PARENTS OURSELVES

[1] Louise Hay, *You Can Heal Your Life* (London: Eden Grove Editions 1988) p. 105.

[2] Nuala O'Faolain, *My Dream of You* (New York: Riverhead Books 2001) pp. 404-5.

CHAPTER 6 – BREAKING THE MOULD

[1] Louise Hay, *You Can Heal Your Life* (London: Eden Grove Editions 1988) pp.40-43.

[2] Ibid., pp. 76-77.

CHAPTER 7 – BODY KNOWING

1. Christiane Northrup, *Women's Bodies, Women's Wisdom* (London: Piatkus 1995) p. 47.
2. Christopher Corthay, aged 6, from a magazine cutting used in a collage.
3. Candace Pert, *Molecules of Emotion* (London: Pocket Books 1999) p. 141.
4. Clarissa Pinkola Estés, *Women Who Run with the Wolves: Myths and Stories of the Wild Woman Archetype* (New York: Ballantine Books 1992) p. 200.
5. Leslie Kenton, *The New Raw Energy* (London: Vermillion 1994); *The Raw Energy Bible* (London: Vermillion 1998).
6. Louise Hay, *You Can Heal Your Life* (London: Eden Grove Editions 1988) Chapter 15.
7. Gill Edwards, *Stepping into the Magic* (London: Judy Piatkus 1993) Chapter 6.
8. Louise Hay, *You Can Heal Your Life* (London: Eden Grove Editions 1988).
9. Gill Edwards, *Stepping into the Magic* (London: Judy Piatkus 1993).
10. Donna Ladkin, *"Talking with Trees: Remembering the Language of Home" ReVision* 23(4) (Bath: 2001) p. 7.

CHAPTER 8 – THE MAGIC OF MENSTRUATION

1. Vicki Noble, *Shakti Woman Feeling our Fire, Healing our World* (New York: HarperCollins 1991) p. 22.
2. Barbara Walker, *The Women's Encyclopedia of Myths and Secrets* (New York: HarperCollins 1983) pp. 669-673; pp. 645-648.
3. Christiane Northrup, *Women's Bodies, Women's Wisdom* (London: Piatkus 1995) p. 97.
4. *We'moon: Gaia Rhythms for Womyn* (Oregon: Mother Tongue Inc.)
5. Clarissa Pinkola Estés, *Women Who Run with the Wolves: Myths and Stories of the Wild Woman Archetype* (New York: Ballantine Books 1992) p. 293.
6. Vicki Noble, *Shakti Woman: Feeling our Fire, Healing our World* (New York: HarperCollins 1991) p. 29.
7. Ibid., p. 14.
8. Lara Owen, *"The Sabbath of Women" Resurgence* No:150, 1992.
9. Kami McBride at www.awakenedwoman.com (April 16 2001).
10. Judith Duerk, *Circle of Stones: Woman's Journey to Herself* (Philadelphia: Innisfree Press 1999) p. 38.
11. Kami McBride at www.awakenedwoman.com (April 16 2001).
12. Lara Owen, *Her Blood is Gold: Reclaiming the Power of Menstruation* (London: Aquarian/Thorsons 1993) p. 24.
13. Ibid., Chapter 7.
14. Luisa Francia, *Dragontime* (Woodstock: Ash Tree Publishing 1991) p. 34.

CHAPTER 9 – WISDOM, SPIRITUALITY AND MENOPAUSE

[1] Lara Owen, *Her Blood is Gold: Reclaiming the Power of Menstruation* (London: Aquarian/Thorsons 1993) p. 45.

[2] Christiane Northrup, *Women's Bodies, Women's Wisdom* (London: Piatkus 1995) p. 95.

[3] Lara Owen, *Her Blood is Gold: Reclaiming the Power of Menstruation* (London: Aquarian/Thorsons 1993) p. 75.

[4] Lara Owen, "The Sabbath of Women" *Resurgence* No:150, 1992.

[5] Luisa Francia, *Dragontime* (Woodstock: Ash Tree Publishing 1991) p. 26.

[6] Vicki Noble, review comments on book cover of Luisa Francia *Dragontime* (Ash Tree Publishing 1991).

[7] Vicki Noble, *Shakti Woman: Feeling our Fire, Healing our World* (New York: HarperCollins 1991) p. 14.

[8] Clarissa Pinkola Estés, *Women Who Run with the Wolves: Myths and Stories of the Wild Woman Archetype* (New York: Ballantine Books 1992) pp. 293-4.

[9] Lara Owen, *Her Blood is Gold: Reclaiming the Power of Menstruation* (London: Aquarian/Thorsons 1993) p. 112.

[10] Ibid., Chapter 3.

[11] Leslie Kenton, *Passage to Power* (London: Vermillion 1998) pp. 67-79.

[12] Christiane Northrup *Women's Bodies, Women's Wisdom* (London: Piatkus 1995) pp. 410-13.

[13] Susun Weed, *Menopausal Years: The Wise Woman Way* (Woodstock: Ash Tree Publishing 1992).

[14] Ibid., p. ix.

[15] Ibid., p. x.

[16] Ibid., pp. 35-6.

[17] Christiane Northrup, *Women's Bodies, Women's Wisdom* (London: Piatkus 1995) pp. 420-1

[18] Ibid., p. 420.

[19] Ibid., p. 423.

[20] Scilla Elworthy, *Power and Sex* (Shaftesbury: Element 1997) p. 117.

[21] Vicki Noble, *Shakti Woman: Feeling our Fire, Healing our World* (New York: HarperCollins 1991) p. 36.

[22] Leslie Kenton, *Passage to Power* (London: Vermillion 1998) pp. 142-144.

CHAPTER 10 – OUR PLACE IN THE NATURAL WORLD

[1] Leslie Kenton, *Journey to Freedom* (London: Thorsons 1999) p. 75.

[2] Information from the Campaign for Dark Skies (CfDS) website at www.dark-skies.org The CfDS is a network of volunteers set up in 1989 by the British Astronomical Association who lobby national and local government to control lighting installations to prevent light being emitted above the horizontal.

[3] Johanna Paungger and Thomas Poppe, *The Art of Timing: The Application of Lunar Cycles in Daily Life* (Saffron Walden: C W Daniel Company Limited 2000).

[4] Deborah Kellaway, ed. *The Illustrated Book of Women Gardeners* (UK: Bullfinch Press, Little, Brown & Company 1997) p. 9.

[5] Ibid., p.32.

[6] Donna Ladkin, *"Talking with Trees: Remembering the Language of Home"* ReVision 23(4) (Bath: 2001) p. 7.

[7] Ibid., p. 1.

[8] Ibid., p. 2.

[9] Ibid., p. 1.

[10] Clarissa Pinkola Estés, *Women Who Run with the Wolves: Myths and Stories of the Wild Woman Archetype* (New York: Ballantine Books 1992) p. 80.

[11] Peter Reason, *Inaugural Lecture: Justice, Sustainability, and Participation* (Bath: 2002) p. 9.

[12] Andy Goldsworthy, *Time* (London: Thames & Hudson 2000).

[13] Simon Rake in *Sarah Gillespie*, produced for exhibition, New Street Gallery, Plymouth. (White Lane Press 2002) p. 3.

[14] Susun Weed, *Wise Woman Herbal: Healing Wise* (New York: Ash Tree Publishing 1998).

[15] Lyall Watson, *Supernature: A Natural History of the Supernatural* (London: Coronet Books 1974) pp. 247-8.

[16] Deborah Kellaway, ed. *The Illustrated Book of Women Gardeners* (UK: Bullfinch Press, Little, Brown & Company 1997) p. 31.

[17] Judith Duerk, *I Sit Listening to the Wind: Woman's Encounter Within Herself* (Philadelphia: Innisfree Press 1999) pp. 20-22.

[18] Ibid., p. 23.

[19] Peter Reason, *Inaugural Lecture: Justice, Sustainability, and Participation* (Bath: 2002) p. 7.

[20] Deborah Kellaway, ed. *The Illustrated Book of Women Gardeners* (UK: Bullfinch Press, Little, Brown & Company 1997) pp. 192-3.

[21] Fritjof Capra, *Uncommon Wisdom* (London: Flamingo 1989) p. 33.

[22] Leslie Kenton, *Journey to Freedom* (London: Thorsons 1999) pp. 62-3.

CHAPTER 11 – THE SILENCE OF WOMEN

[1] Sheila Rowbotham, *"Women's Consciousness, Man's World"* (1973) in Humm (ed.) *Feminisms: A Reader* (Hemel Hempstead: Harvester Wheatsheaf 1992).

[2] Chris Mahony, *"Glass Ceiling as Tough"* People Management, 12th October 2000.

[3] People Management, 8th December 2001, p. 9.

[4] Alison Eadie, *"Powerful women, glass ceilings ... and baby talk"* Daily Telegraph Business News, July 5th 2001.

[5] Leslie Kenton, *Passage to Power* (London: Vermillion 1998) p. 288.

[6] Paul Newham, *The Singing Cure: An Introduction to Voice Movement Therapy* (London: Rider 1993) pp. 236-7.

[7] Angela Carter, *The Magic Toyshop* (London: Virago 1981).

[8] Clarissa Pinkola Estés, *Women Who Run With the Wolves: Myths and Stories of the Wild Woman Archetype* (New York: Ballantine Books 1992) p. 374.

[9] Ibid., p. 158.

[10] Ibid., p.378.

[11] Donna Ladkin, *An Invitation to a Co-operative Inquiry* (unpublished paper: January 2003).

[12] Louise Hay, *You Can Heal Your Life* (London: Eden Grove Editions 1988).

[13] Gill Edwards, *Stepping into the Magic* (London: Judy Piatkus 1993).

[14] Caroline Myss, *Anatomy of the Spirit: The Seven Stages of Power and Healing* (London: Bantam Books 1997).

[15] Mary Field Belenky, Blythe McVicker Clinchy, Nancy Rule Goldberger and Jill Mattuck Tarule, *Women's Ways of Knowing: The Development of Self, Voice, and Mind* (New York: BasicBooks 1986) p. 146.

[16] Marianne Williamson, *Return to Love* (London: Thorsons 1992) p. 191.

[17] Mary Field Belenky, Blythe McVicker Clinchy, Nancy Rule Goldberger and Jill Mattuck Tarule, *Women's Ways of Knowing: The Development of Self, Voice, and Mind* (New York: BasicBooks 1986) p. 18.

[18] Melissa Harris, *A Wise Woman* (1995) in *We'moon: Gaia Rhythms for Womyn* (Oregon: Mother Tongue Inc.1998) Moon VI.

[19] Christina Baldwin, *Life's Companion* (New York: Bantam Books 1991) p. 47.

[20] John Fox, *Finding What You Didn't Lose* (New York: Tarcher/Putnam 1995) p. 11.

[21] Clarissa Pinkola Estés, *Women Who Run with the Wolves: Myths and Stories of the Wild Woman Archetype* (New York: Ballantine Books 1992) pp. 27-8.

CHAPTER 12 – MAKING A SONG AND DANCE

[1] The words of this song were written in the 1970s and are credited to Aidan Kelly and C. Taleisin Edwards. It is probably an adaptation of a hymn with similar wording written in 1963 by Sydney Carter, of which Stainer & Bell Ltd. are the copyright holders.

[2] Wendy Buonaventura, *Serpent of the Nile: Women and Dance in the Arab World* (London: Saqi Books 1994) p. 26.

[3] Paul Newham, *The Singing Cure: An Introduction to Voice Movement Therapy* (London: Rider 1993) p. 21.

[4] Wendy Buonaventura, *Serpent of the Nile: Women and Dance in the Arab World* (London: Saqi Books 1994) p. 160.

[5] Jean Houston, *The Possible Human* (Los Angeles: Tarcher 1982) p. xix.

[6] Morris Berman, *Coming To Our Senses: Body and Spirit in the Hidden History of the West* (New York: Bantam New Age) p. 318.

[7] Ropes Challenge Course, run by CHC Ltd for private and corporate clients, described as follows: "a developmental process and strictly 'challenge by choice'. This means, within the safety constraints, you choose what to do and how you do it." Sadie praised both the discipline of safety procedures and the consistent attention to reflective learning. The course is run by Suzie Morel who can be reached by email at: corporate_health_consultants@compuserve.com

[8] Wendy Buonaventura, *Serpent of the Nile: Women and Dance in the Arab World* (London: Saqi Books 1994) p. 25.

[9] Ibid., Chapter 1. p. 25.

[10] Matthew Fox, *A Spirituality Named Compassion* (New York: HarperCollins 1990) pp. 41-44.

[11] Jill Purce, *The Mystic Spiral: Journey of the Soul* (London: Thames & Hudson 1974) pp. 30-31.

[12] Fritjof Capra, *The Tao of Physics* (London: Flamingo 1983) p. 269.

[13] Jill Purce, *The Healing Voice:* workshop flier, 1996.

[14] Paul Newham, *The Singing Cure: An Introduction to Voice Movement Therapy* (London: Rider 1993) pp. 13-14.

[15] Ibid., book jacket.

[16] Gabrielle Roth, *Sweat Your Prayers: Movement as Spiritual Practice* (Newleaf, 1999).

[17] Clarissa Pinkola Estés, *Women Who Run with the Wolves: Myths and Stories of the Wild Woman Archetype* (New York: Ballantine Books 192) p. 339.

[18] *Psychological Review* 2000 July; 107(3): pp. 411-29.

ABOUT THE AUTHOR

Jill Treseder feels passionately that women, men and the planet need more of the understanding and behaviour that can be short-handed as 'feminine'. Jill has been involved in encouraging a more feminine style of management in organisations of all sizes and shapes for the last twenty years. In that time she has been a member of some ten women's groups meeting to read and critique books; to support each other professionally; to share ritual, healing and sacred drama; to write and to dance; and simply to 'be' together. She has been a closet writer since she was seven years old.

Jill is active in the roles of daughter, mother and grandmother amongst others. She lives with her husband in Devon, where she is part of a lively village community.

Jill sees the process of publishing this book and of drawing all these threads together into a coherent identity as part of her own ongoing spiral to wholeness.

WORKSHOPS FOR

the wise WOMAN within

Using her extensive experience of group facilitation,
Jill has developed a workshop alongside her book.

The Wise Woman Within workshop can run as a short taster,
a whole day or for longer as required.

Workshops are offered for women who are at different
stages of their exploration or wanting to focus on different
aspects of using inner wisdom.

For example:
Getting to Know your Wise Woman
Charting the territory
Striking up an acquaintance
Making plans to meet again
Making a Friend of your Wise Woman
In depth exploration of chosen themes
Integrating the wise woman into your life
Making new approaches and skills your own
Taking your Wise Woman to Work
Identifying conflicts and challenges
Mapping a creative strategy
Finding a language

**To find out more and to make a booking,
visit the StarDrum website at:**
www.stardrum.com

PRAISE FOR *THE WISE WOMAN WITHIN*

"A warm, honest, intelligent account of one woman's search for her own creativity, emotional freedom and authentic power. Jill Treseder writes of the most important journey any of us ever take - the journey towards coming to know who we really are. Her book is an important contribution to the growing body of work attempting to chart it."

Leslie Kenton, shamanic practitioner, healthy living expert,
author of *Passage to Power* and *Journey to Freedom*.

"This appealing and informative handbook should be found on every woman's nightstand; it should be required reading in science classes everywhere. With great care and intelligence, the reader is initiated into a more conscious and sensuous way of relating to the experience of being a woman — from childhood through the menopausal journey. The personal voice of the author is supported and expanded by additional voices of other women sharing their experiences, thoughts, and feelings about everything in a woman's life from the shocking sight of the first blood to the myriad ways women allow ourselves to be silenced. Exciting, fresh, and extremely useful — get the book, organize a group of women or girls, and begin!"

Vicki Noble, feminist shaman healer, co-creator of Motherpeace,
author of *Shakti Woman: Feeling our Fire, Healing our World* and
The Double Goddess: Women Sharing Power.

"A very comprehensive and well researched book. Re-connecting with our feminine wisdom is just the tonic we women need after half a century of liberation struggle in a man's world."

Gael Lindenfield, psychotherapist, self-help expert, best-selling writer,
author of *Managing Anger* and *The Self-Esteem Bible*.

StarDrum
Turning the World Upside-Down!

with
StarDrum Books
For the books you thought you'd never see!

— Dedicated to —
Consciousness Expansion · Human Potential
Self-Empowerment · Personal Responsibility

www.stardrum.com

books@stardrum.com
Books · CDs · Videos · DVDs